TYRANNICIDE

By Dr. Evan Keliher

Pedagogue Press P.O. Box 28808 San Diego, CA 92198

ISBN: 978-0-9648859-0-5
SAN: 298-8054

Library of Congress Catalog
Card Number: 2007943693

Printed in the United States of America

OTHER WORKS BY EVAN KELIHER

BOOKS

BOOMERS!
(A Survival Guide for the Future)

Grandpa's Marijuana Handbook

Guerrilla Warfare for Teachers

The De-Balling of America

Grandpa Ganja's High School Survival Guide

VIDEOS/FILMS

Rebel High *(feature film)*
Montreal, Canada

My Lovely Bank *(sitcom pilot)*
Montreal, Canada

Grandpa's Marijuana Handbook *(the movie)*
San Diego, CA

STAGE PLAYS

Sandwiched Light
Witte's End

See additional plays/screenplays/sitcoms
www.grandpaspotbook.com

"…Governments are instituted among Men, deriving their just powers from the consent of the governed, — That whenever any Form of Government becomes destructive of these ends, it is the Right of the People to alter or to abolish it, and to institute new Government, laying its foundation on such principles and organizing its powers in such form, as to them shall seem most likely to effect their Safety and Happiness."

The Declaration of Independence

PROLOGUE

The Butterfly Syndrome avers that a single flap of a butterfly's wing over the Indian Ocean could set air currents in motion that would eventually produce a hurricane in the Caribbean. While such an event isn't likely to occur, the concept is a valid one in that an accumulation of insignificant and isolated acts can and often do produce extraordinary results in unexpected ways.

Accordingly, a nation is more than the sum of its parts; it is a living organism with its own heart and brain and capable of acting in a singular manner when threatened by outside forces. While slow to recognize danger and even slower to respond, the body politic, dozing in Plato's cave, watches shadow play in the media and only grudgingly absorbs signals, half-listens to rumors and innuendos, and relies more on intuition than reason to move itself to action. However, once decided it can move with dispatch and daring in righting perceived wrongs.

In brief, the United States is a far cry from the country it was following WWII. The nation became divided, the political parties more partisan, wealth grew for the few as living standards fell for average Americans, and a sense of unease settled over the land. In the background, murmuring softly, the equivalent of a butterfly's wing fluttered and the heart of the organism felt it and the brain stirred itself as understanding came and a call for action made itself heard.

This is an account of the events that followed, as recounted by an eyewitness.

CHAPTER ONE

Sen. Hiram Biggers (R-GA), a porcine man with slits for eyes and the greedy nature of the pig, actually owned several pig farms and regularly sought more pork of a different kind to increase the value of his own. His colleagues even referred to him as Hiram the Ham Guy and generously voted for his pork in exchange for his votes for theirs. Biggers managed to accumulate a significant fortune over the years and a good deal of power in Congress by arranging deals that would make Machiavelli green with envy.

In short, Hiram Biggers was a conniving fraud plunked down in a sea of frauds so crooked they could hide behind corkscrews. He never had a thought for his fellow man, cared nothing for the poor; in fact, he opposed every bill that in any way benefited them and for every bill that caused them harm. All of his conniving, fraudulent colleagues did the same.

And so it happened one warm day in late spring that Sen. Hiram Biggers spoke on behalf of his bill to eliminate the inheritance tax and thereby add billions to the coffers of the rich who had paid the senator in kind for his services.

"...really benefits everybody," he intoned in his gravelly, down home style, "because it all trickles down, don't you see? People need money to invest in new factories and buildings and research and that means more jobs for everybody. That's how these folks would use the extra money to improve the economy and help in the war on terrorism and make America a safer place, too.

"It boils down to patriotism, don't you see? I tell you it's un-American for the government to have confiscatory taxes. Why, if they can seize more from the rich today, what's to stop 'em from seizing more from you tomorrow? It's all about American values, my friends, and it's time we all stood up for American values."

No one in the chamber paid attention to the senator's speech, as the matter under discussion had already been decided in clandestine meetings with key players. The votes necessary for the eventual passage of still another law intended to profit the rich at the expense of the poor and middle class were safely in and accounted for before Biggers took the stage.

Biggers stepped away from the rostrum and was met by a clutch of fellow conspirators who shook his hand and patted his back and said good things about his performance and their collective success. It was a scene reminiscent of one that occurred when Brutus exchanged high fives over Caesar's corpse in the well of the Roman senate.

Flushed with still another victory the senator went back to his office to pick up the envelope stuffed with cash that he knew would be waiting for him and headed for home. At 3:14 exactly he pulled into a downtown-parking garage, climbed out, and started for the exit. At 3:26 he was found between parked cars with a neat, round hole in his forehead and quite dead.

Of course, the media were delighted. Always starved for meaningful fare, or even fare not so meaningful, every TV channel blared the news in a seemingly endless rush of so-called breaking stories that continued to break for days without ever shedding any new light on the matter.

The facts were actually few and simple. Minutes after the paramedics arrived the F.B.I. was on the scene along with some C.I.A. types and a host of local cops to control bystanders. Yellow tape closed off the entire parking structure and crowds returning to their cars quickly formed up and added to the confusion.

Teams of F.B.I. agents scoured the structure for evidence and all they found was a single ejected .22-caliber shell casing on the floor a few feet from the body. At first glance it appeared to be a robbery but the senator still had the cash-filled envelope in his coat pocket and an $8,000 Rolex on his wrist.

In fact, there were no real clues to be found. No fingerprints or cigarette butts, no blood or saliva or hair for possible DNA samples. Biggers' clean fingernails, unstained clothing, and neatly combed hair all indicated there'd been no struggle, that the attack had been very fast and unexpected. The killer must have intended to kill Biggers from the start in what had all the markings of a professional hit by the mob, but that theory raised the question of why since there was no record of any mob dealings with the senator.

The authorities released no details of the crime in an attempt to conceal how little evidence they had, but they floated the story that it was a robbery gone wrong, that the killer was probably interrupted and fled before he could rob his victim.

This story was not chosen randomly but only

after much careful thought. Any other version might reflect badly on the senator or on the Senate itself since everyone knew Biggers was a cheap crook and linked to his fellow crooks by an intricate network that could put the lot of them in the big house for decades.

Many were even glad that Biggers didn't have a chance to utter any sort of deathbed confession that might redound to their harm. It often happens that arrested scoundrels will blow the whistle on their accomplices in an effort to avoid a lengthy sojourn in the slammer and no one doubted that Hiram would have sung like a drunk in a karaoke bar.

On the following Monday Bob Ingersoll crossed the city room of the Sentinel with a fresh cup of coffee and half a cruller and sat down at his desk. A lanky 6'2" and slim, Bob disliked making hard choices early in the day so he simplified things by wearing what amounted to a uniform. He wore custom jeans with $90 button-down oxford dress shirts, Allen Edmond loafers, and a sport coat from Hickey Freeman. He liked to dress for comfort but not at the expense of style and class.

The day's mail had arrived, a total of two letters, and he turned to it with a will. Where the mail once involved a dozen or more letters, real paper and envelopes and stamps, it had morphed into e-mail, a good or bad development depending on one's point of view. In former times one had to assemble writing paper, envelopes, stamps, bottles of Wite Out, pens/ pencils/crayons, and possess basic writing skills before writing the first word.

With e-mail any half-wit can bang out some

ungrammatical crap on a keyboard in seconds and send it worldwide without a trip to the post office. As a result, almost nobody can write literate English nowadays. E-mail and text messages have no need for grammar, coherence, spelling, punctuation, careful thought. It is a great loss, greater than we know.

Still, the occasional old-fashioned letter showed up and Bob always regarded each one as something special, a link to other times. Most were not special and came from people without computers, of course, but at least they were real paper and felt good in one's hands.

Bob sipped the coffee, took a bite of the cruller, and opened the first one. A single page of stationery contained the words: "It wasn't robbery." It was signed with the letter K. He turned the letter over and peeked in the envelope and even shook it to no avail. It was postmarked from Atlanta with a return address in Las Vegas. He looked up, brow furrowed in thought. Synapses snapped, axons fizzed, dendrites lit up neurons in a wild electrical shower of sparks and in seconds Bob analyzed the data and reached a sound conclusion.

"A crank," he thought, "some asshole playing detective." He tossed letter and envelope into the wastebasket and reached for the second one. Forty-five minutes later he sighed mightily, closed drawers, turned off the computer, and spotted the letter in the wastebasket. He hesitated, shrugged, retrieved letter and envelope and tossed them onto his desk as he left.

As Bob drove to his condo across the Potomac the investigations continued at all levels from the Senate chambers to lowly police precincts and none turned up a single new clue or even a new slant that was based on anything more than rumor or speculation. However, an observer might have noticed that most members of Congress looked over their shoulders with more frequency than usual.

Several senators met that evening in the conference room of Majority Leader Tom Hoskins to discuss Biggers' death and reassure themselves as to its likely consequences. Max Abbott (R-MI) and Ted Pastor (R-TX) were co-sponsors of Biggers' inheritance tax bill and also recipients of cash-filled envelopes. As Friday was payoff day they knew that Biggers had one in his pocket when killed and they feared a possible link to them. Hoskins didn't know about the envelopes of cash but he would not have been surprised to learn of them, as he was himself a crook.

After all, who among them wasn't similarly encumbered much of the time? Any unannounced search of a congressman's briefcase or inside coat pocket or even his home freezer would reveal like caches of greenbacks that couldn't be accounted for by Mandrake the Magician. It seems it isn't a bad thing to have such tainted monies; it's just not a good idea to get caught with them.

"…it was a robbery," Pastor said.

"That's what everybody's saying," Hoskins agreed.

"Sure, some two-bit hood with a gun," Abbott said. "Probably a drug addict."

Pastor agreed. "This town's full of 'em. You're not safe anywhere nowadays. D.C. has more armed people than Baghdad, for God's sake."

"Yeah, why is that?" Hoskins said. "This town is a gun-free zone. Nobody can buy a gun here or even own one, it seems. How come everybody in town is a goddamn walking arsenal?"

"Maybe somebody told 'em about the Second Amendment," Abbott said.

"Well, look, it's too bad about Hiram but it's just one of those unfortunate things that happen to people," Hoskins said. "It could have been any of us. He was in the wrong place at the wrong time, is all. It was a random thing. We've got to move on here."

"The funeral's tomorrow."

"Yeah. Noon at the National Cathedral."

"Wasn't Hiram a Catholic?"

"Hell, no. He was a goddamn heathen. You could bury him in a landfill and it wouldn't make any difference to him."

"What the hell, it was good enough for Mozart," Pastor said.

The others nodded agreement and so did the rest of Congress. Everyone supported the robbery theory, as it was the most palatable one that could be digested with fewest side effects. The authorities aided and abetted the theorists by withholding information and encouraging the media to run with it. Since that was the only story propounded, it was adopted by almost everyone and generally accepted as what happened to the luckless senator. In point of fact, based on the evidence given, no other conclusion was likely.

Biggers' funeral was held the next day at the National Cathedral and since Bob had two tickets to cover the proceedings he took fashion page editor

Colleen Quinn with him. She was tall and svelte and looked like a fashion editor with clothes that seemed to come from the pages of Elle or Vogue. Even better, she had a razor-sharp mind and a sense of independence that would have pleased Ayn Rand.

Some might call their outing a date but it actually wasn't. They'd known each other for a decade and had an early fling that continued sporadically even into the present. Everything considered it was an ideal relationship that worked on many levels, as they'd become sound friends and confidants.

On the way into the Cathedral distraught ticket seekers offered Bob $500 for his ducats but he stayed true to the journalist's pledge and resolutely refused to compromise his integrity. Besides, it would mean filing a phony story on an assignment he'd not covered and that really would be an affront to his code of ethics.

The funeral was a marvelous display of pomp and circumstance that was not unlike a graduation ceremony with a dirge replacing Elgar's famous march. Everyone of note showed up to mourn or gloat depending on his past relationship with the departed. The gloaters far exceeded the mourners, as is usually the case with the funerals of political figures.

The president spoke glowingly of Biggers' fine character, wisdom, and compassion, and obvious snickers were heard in the great room. When the president declared that Biggers was a "… righteous man, a man of honor…" a voice in the gallery sang out, "Oh, my God!" and the speaker threw an arm up in a defensive posture to ward off the lightning bolts he knew had to be en route.

Bach resounded in the vast room, a large choir rendered several numbers in Latin, and no less a figure than the Cardinal himself sprayed the audience with holy water as he led a procession down the main aisle. Some said the holy water spat and sizzled like water hitting a hot skillet when it landed on politicians in the audience, but those stories may be apocryphal.

All in all, it was a grand affair that received good reviews in the press and talk of an Emmy for the TV coverage. Many were heard to wish that another senator would be gunned down so they could have as much fun again. Hiram the Ham Guy would have been impressed with the show.

Bob and Colleen remained in their seats to avoid the jammed aisles and watched mourners and gloaters file out of the cavernous church in a slowly moving river of humanity. Most talked amiably to friends, laughing, arranging lunch dates or trysts with thoughts of poor Hiram vanished from their minds even before they'd left the premises.

Commenting on their gay mood, Colleen said, "You'd think it was just another social affair."

"It was. They come to be seen. Nobody gives a rap about the Ham Guy."

"They could at least pretend, couldn't they?"

"Why? To deceive each other?"

"Why not? Maybe they could trick themselves into thinking they're compassionate, caring people. That might raise their level of consciousness."

"They're all rich; they don't need to be conscious."

"Fuck 'em. Let's get some lunch."

"Now you've raised my level of consciousness."

They stood and slipped into the thinning crowd and mini-stepped their way out into the bright midday sunlight and gave themselves over to deciding on where to eat. They settled on a small Italian restaurant famous for its pasta and conveniently nearby. Ten minutes later they chose vegetarian lasagna from the menu, thick slices of pumpernickel bread, and a carafe of Cabernet to round out a meal that would be fit for a king if one happened by.

Wine in hand, they settled back to wait for lunch.

"So, what's the real story on Biggers' death?"

"A robbery. A street crime."

"Says who?"

"Everybody. The feds, cops, witnesses…"

"What witnesses?"

"Not witnesses, reporters. Welsh for one. He was there and saw the crime scene up close."

"I didn't hear any evidence that supported a robbery. How would they know that?" She paused and looked steadily him. "You know something, don't you?"

"Me? No. What? I only know what everybody else knows."

"It wasn't a robbery, was it?"

"No comment."

"Then it wasn't."

Bob sighed heavily. "Okay, it probably wasn't a robbery. Welsh said Biggers was wearing a Rolex. If it was robbery the guy would at least get that watch. They have no idea what actually happened."

"So what's next?"

"More investigations. You can't shoot a U.S. senator

and just forget about it, not unless you don't mind a lot of pissed-off politicians on your ass."

"In other words, it's more of the same, then."

"It's depressing, isn't it?"

Colleen leaned in for her wine glass and her gaping blouse revealed cleavage that would get her employment as a Victoria's Secret model. "Maybe I could cheer you up a bit," she said

Bob eyed her perky, braless breasts and grinned. "You already have," he said.

"You're easy."

"And you're glad."

She smiled a soft woman's smile and put her hand on his. "We're both glad."

The waiter appeared then and they turned their attention to the piping hot lasagna and fell silent because their mouths were stopped with pasta and bread awash in red wine. Colleen had to get back to work and so did Bob, but an assignation was arranged for that evening in order to finish what they'd started at lunch.

CHAPTER TWO

The morning after the funeral Bob woke from his tryst with the fair Colleen and found he'd neglected to go home last night. It was eight a.m. and it was clamor from the kitchen that awakened him. By the time he'd had a go at his toilet and arrived in the kitchen Colleen was putting the finishing touches on an elegant omelet complete with wheat toast and sliced melon. Bob wondered if she was baiting a trap of some sort.

"Are you baiting a trap of some sort?" he asked, his speech slightly garbled because his mouth was full of elegant omelet.

"To catch what? You? All I have to do is show my boobs and I can do with you as I will."

"Ah, too true," Bob said, sighing. "I am a man of deep passion."

"What passion? You're just horny."

"Yeah, you're right."

"But that's not an indictment, you know."

They looked at each other and both laughed.

Minutes later, Bob cleared the breakfast debris away while Colleen dressed and they left together. Once outside, he kissed her and said, "See you on Friday."

"Have a nice trip."

Colleen went to work and Bob headed home to pack for an assignment in Miami that would keep him away until Friday afternoon. While he was gone he was able to keep abreast of the Biggers matter because it was still all over the media even though there was never anything new to report. The robbery theory held sway and it began to appear that would end up the official conclusion. But then he returned from assignment on Friday afternoon and caught up on the mail accumulated during his absence and matters changed dramatically.

Aside from the usual e-mail there was a single letter waiting for him and it had a familiar look about it, a case of postal déjà vu. The return address read Las Vegas again but it was mailed from Baltimore a day earlier. He opened the envelope carefully and found an identical sheet of paper that also contained but a single sentence. It read: ".22 caliber. Think Sarajevo."

No churning mental machinery on this one. Bob scooped up the first letter lying on his desk and headed for editor Pete Schevo's office.

He entered unannounced and said, "Give this a gander!"

Pete took the letters and read them. "Jesus Christ!"

"What do you think?"

"Did the cops say it was a .22?"

"No. Just that he was shot. I got it from Carl. He overheard the cops talking about it."

"Hmm. Could it be a guess?"

"Not likely."

"Sarajevo. Archduke Ferdinand. WWI. What's that mean?"

"An assassination?"

"Terrorists?"

Bob shrugged. "If it was terrorists I'd say it was an assassination. If it was a pissed-off husband maybe just the usual murder."

Pete studied the letters, turned them over, held them to the light. "We have to give 'em to the feds. It may be nothing but we can't take a chance. If it turns out to be terrorists planning to blow up the Capitol the feds will want a heads-up on it."

"Probably just a crank."

"But a crank who knows what kind of gun was used."

"That's true."

"Okay. We call it in."

Pete phoned the F.B.I. office and reported the letters. He was told to wait for an agent and he didn't have long to wait. Four agents showed up so fast that the editor looked dazedly around to see if they'd been hiding in a nearby closet.

Agent Jim Scanlon was the lead agent and it was apparent from his manner that he was in charge. Newly arrived at the D.C office, he was a big, gruff man with the bulk of a slightly out of shape linebacker and anxious to score a major success by solving Biggers' death posthaste. Dominating the scene, he took in the room and its contents in a single glance and focused on the editor.

"You got a letter on the Biggers case?"

Pete shook his head. "I'm the editor. Pete Schevo. Bob got the letter."

He turned to Bob. "You have the letter?"

"Yes. Both of them."

"There are two letters?"

Bob handed him the letters. "The first one came on Monday. The second came today."

Scanlon read the brief messages and looked up at Bob. "Why didn't you report the first one?"

"I thought it was a crank. It didn't connect until the second one mentioned the gun. I knew that information hadn't been released."

"How did you know about the gun?"

"A friend overheard the cops talking about it."

"Did you tell anyone else about the gun? The caliber?"

Bob shook his head. "No."

"Who was this friend?"

Bob looked at the editor and raised a quizzical eyebrow. Pete nodded.

"Carl Welsh. He's a reporter here."

Scanlon turned to Pete. "Is he here? I need to talk to him."

"He's on assignment…"

"Call him."

"He's on his way to…"

"Get him."

Pete shrugged and picked up the phone. Scanlon bit his lip and assumed a thoughtful mien while his fellow agents gazed stoically and awaited orders. The editor's voice filled the room.

"Helen? Call Welsh and tell him to come home. I know, it doesn't matter, just tell him." He hung up and looked to Scanlon.

More lip biting. He examined the letters as though looking for fingerprints or traces of anthrax. Crossing to a window he stared out at the traffic below and then reread the letters. After a moment, he turned to Bob and said, "Why do you think these were sent to you?"

"I don't know. Maybe because they know me from my column."

"Do you own a .22 caliber gun?"

"No. I have a gun but it's a .32 caliber Beretta Tomcat."

"Why do you have a gun?"

"Why does anyone have a gun?"

"Do you have it with you?"

"No. I don't carry it as a rule."

"When do you carry it?"

"When I think there's a chance I might need it."

"Hmm."

Bob wasn't sure if that was reassuring or not.

After reflecting for a moment longer, Scanlon handed the letters to one of the agents and turned back to Bob and Pete. "We've got a dead senator, gentlemen. That's not good. Means a lot of pressure. If it's a simple robbery some of the heat will dissipate, but if it's anything else we'll have the entire Congress on our ass."

"What else might it be?" Pete asked.

Scanlon shrugged. "Revenge. Maybe somebody didn't like him…"

"That makes it easy," Bob said. "Look for a guy wearing a blue collar. Every working man in the country hated the bastard."

"I take it you didn't like much him, either," Scanlon said.

"As I said, he was an asshole."

"Bob's right," Pete said. "Dying is the best thing he ever did for the country. Now, if somebody would just shoot a dozen more of his friends, why…"

"So, you had a motive, did you?" Scanlon said.

"Who, me?" Pete said.

"We're looking for suspects, you know."

Pete shook his head. "I'm allergic to guns. I don't even believe in the Second Amendment."

"Neither does the Supreme Court," Bob said ruefully.

Scanlon took a final look around the room as though checking for any overlooked clues. He nodded to the agents and turned toward the door and then turned back.

"Give us a call if you get any more letters, Bob. And don't talk about the case. It's not a gag order. Just give us a few days to see what else develops."

"But we're running a story today on it," Pete said.

"That's okay, just don't include anything we said here. We don't want to tip our hand."

"You don't have much of a hand to tip, do you?" Bob said. "You don't know anything for sure…"

"Nobody knows what we know and we want to keep it like that," Scanlon said curtly. "It's better that way."

"It's okay," Pete said, "mum's the word."

"Mum it is," Bob said.

"Good." He nodded and left with his retinue close behind. Pete looked at Bob and Bob looked back.

"Jesus Christ, we may have an inside track on the story of the year!" Pete said.

"Yeah, and we can't print a word of it."

"No big deal. They can't gag us forever."

"I'm not so sure. If they call it national security or say it's against the Patriot Act we're screwed."

"Right now, sure, but the First Amendment has to kick in there somewhere. The feds can only keep the lid on for so long with that secrecy crap."

"Are you kidding? The bastards can call us terrorists and ship us off to Gitmo and we'll never be heard from again. Have you read the Patriot Act? They even killed habeas corpus. The average illegal immigrant has more civil rights now than we do, for Christ's sake."

Both men fell silent as both suddenly entertained the same thought.

"You don't suppose…?"

Pete hesitated then said thoughtfully, "I don't know."

"Holy shit!"

"Yeah. The story of the century."

And they left it at that. Pete went back to editing and Bob commenced work on next day's column while the wheels of justice rolled with a distant rumbling as various law enforcement agencies geared up for an all-out effort to solve the case that could turn out to be the story of the century.

CHAPTER THREE

Agent Scanlon took the elevator up from the parking garage and made his way through the hallways of the fortress-like headquarters of the F.B.I. The building was designed to withstand an all-out attack by superpowers from this or any other galaxy, although the occupants were not safe from each other as intrigue and sinister machinations filled the air. The building was a place that housed power and the powerful, a combination that always encourages an ongoing struggle for control.

Scanlon arrived at the office of the Director, one Norman Slinker, a man just this side of fifty with a bald pate and bushy eyebrows to compensate for the missing hair. Like Scanlon, he was big but out of shape with a paunch that would serve an alderman well. He concealed the paunch beneath a $3,000 suit.

Scanlon entered and waited for Slinker to finish a phone call. He put the phone down and looked up.

"What?"

"The plot thickens on the Biggers case, sir." He handed him the letters. "These were received at the Sentinel."

Slinker took the letters and read them. "Are these from the killer?"

"We don't know. It's somebody who knows details that weren't released to the public."

Slinker studied the letters again. "Shit."

"It may be the killer is taunting us, sir."

"Maybe. Look, go arrest somebody. Anybody. Bring 'em in for questioning. Just say we have a person of interest—whatever the hell that means. Don't mention terrorists. When somebody knocks off a U.S senator we have to come up with answers pretty damn quick."

"We don't want to mention the letters?"

"No. Fuck the letters. They just complicate things. It's probably a nut case, anyway. We're looking for a lone gunman, a stick-up man who probably has a record for armed robbery. Anything else and it gets tricky. We don't want tricky, Scanlon. We want a nice, open and shut case without any complications like cryptic letters and foreign intrigue. Is that clear?"

"Uh, sir, they found $10,000 in the senator's pocket and he was wearing a Rolex worth $8,000..."

"So?"

"Sir, it couldn't have been robbery if…"

"The robber was in a hurry. Maybe somebody was coming and scared him off before he could search Biggers. Jesus, Scanlon, get with it. It was a goddamn robbery until we decide it wasn't."

"Yes, sir. I'll get right on it."

He reached the door when Slinker stopped him. "Scanlon, I want you to report directly to me on this. Just in case."

"Yes, sir."

Slinker picked up the letters and leaned back to study them as Scanlon closed the door. He looked up and gazed absently into the middle distance while different scenarios played themselves out in his head. None of them had a happy ending.

The authorities did not release the letters in their news briefings largely because they would run counter to the semi-official position that the crime was a robbery and that the police would soon have the murderer(s) in custody. In fact, the F.B.I. had arrested two known armed robbers as persons of interest as Director Slinker had suggested to Scanlon earlier. Neither man could remotely be linked to Biggers as both had strong alibis, but that was a mere detail since they were intended as show suspects and would be released eventually in any case.

Agent Scanlon had followed up by interviewing Carl Welsh regarding his comments on the caliber of the gun but that lead nowhere since he hadn't told anyone other than Bob. While never a certainty that a leak hadn't spread, it was felt that the writer of the letters had to have some connection with the event in order to know such never published details.

The forensics people went over the letters with everything from simple magnifying glasses to electron microscopes and proved conclusively that paper and envelope were entirely bereft of clues. Any office supply store would carry the exact brands. The envelope was sealed with Scotch tape rather than spittle to avoid DNA clues, the same return address on both envelopes led to a vacant lot in Las Vegas, and the stamp was a self-adhesive type. Any clues from the letters would have to originate with the written messages.

Scanlon was able to reach the same conclusion once forensics had submitted its report and he set about doing just that. He called for a meeting with his top aides with but a single item on the agendum, to wit: What does it mean?

They assembled in Scanlon's office at a large conference table and filled half of its ten seats with five of the best minds in the Bureau. They were cunning men, clever and properly devious, men who had gone up against some of the sharpest minds in the underworld and knew all the tricks of the trickiest of them.

Agent Scanlon surveyed his colleagues coolly, measured the cut of their jibs with a practiced eye, and was pleased with what he saw. He opened a manila folder, took out copies of the letters, and handed them to each man. They read the letters and looked up at Scanlon quizzically.

"Well?" Scanlon said.

"Uh, I'm not sure…" Fisby said uncertainly.

"Maybe it's a code…" Ogilvy said.

"Beats me," MacTavish said.

"It could be a red herring to throw us off the track," opined Chilson.

"What track?" Scanlon demanded.

"Uh, the one leading to the real killer?"

"You mean the robber?"

Fisby raised a hesitant hand. "You know, it may be it wasn't a robbery at all."

"Oh, it's a robbery, all right," Chilson said. "The Chief said so."

"But do armed robbers usually send letters to the police after they kill somebody?" MacTavish said.

Scanlon rubbed his chin thoughtfully. "And not just any letters but one that refers to Sarajevo."

"That's right," Fisby said, "how many guys ever even heard of Sarajevo? I say the one who wrote those letters was an educated guy, maybe a professional man, not the kind of guy that goes around committing street crimes."

"And where does that leave us?" Scanlon said.

"We know it wasn't a simple robbery," Ogilvy said.

"And what does that mean?"

"It means it was something else."

"The usual. Angry husband."

"A jealous lover."

"Revenge from somebody Biggers fucked over."

"Or terrorists," Scanlon said. "Or suicide or an accident or a serial killer…"

"Are there any other clues?" Fisby said.

"The caliber of the gun," MacTavish said. "Pros use small caliber guns like that. Less noise, smoke. Maybe it was a professional hit."

"But why?" Chilson said. "Mob guys don't shoot senators; they mostly shoot each other."

"How about this?" Ogilvy said, leaning forward. "We know Biggers was a crook. Friday was payoff day and that ten grand was graft. Maybe he took a bribe, didn't deliver on it, and kept the cash. The guy got pissed and…"

"That makes more sense than a straight mob hit."

"Yeah, anybody can hire a hit man."

"It's a good theory," Scanlon said, "but so are all the others." He bit his lip some more. "So we work all of 'em. Follow up on every single angle no matter how unlikely it is. Put teams out there 24/7. Interview everybody. If we can at least find the motive we'll know what we're up against here. Until then, we don't even know what it is we're looking for."

They rose as one and started out.

"Right, Jim!"

"Good plan!"

"The bastard's as good as caught!"

Left alone, Scanlon frowned, bit his lip, and said aloud, "I'm not so fucking sure about that."

It had been a week since Biggers' funeral and, while the Bureau was more worried with each passing day, the politicians in the Capitol proved the old adage about things out of sight being forgotten. Though still somewhat uneasy most of them quickly resumed business as usual as lobbyists filled the lobbies, deals were made, envelopes passed covertly in backrooms, and Hiram the Ham Guy hurtled toward obscurity. There is little room for sentiment in politicians as such an emotion could lead to humanitarian thoughts and patriotism and a love of country that would likely interfere with the hard business of selling one's soul at regular intervals.

Even Bob found the dearth of news drew his attention from Biggers to other matters in spite of the fact that he'd been more involved in the case than just about anybody else. With the passage of time it appeared that the crime would soon be written off as an unsolved street robbery and filed away with all the other unsolved crimes in the cops' voluminous files.

A week after the letters arrived and four days of increased activity by his top aides and their 24/7 investigations proved fruitless, Scanlon dropped by the Sentinel with a new tactic he hoped would be more productive.

Bob was on the phone when Scanlon appeared at his cubicle and he quickly cut the call short.

"Don't tell me," he said. "You caught the killer."

"No such luck."

"You need luck to catch crooks?"

"It helps. Get any more letters?"

"Not even a postcard."

"How was the funeral?"

"Very entertaining. They made Biggers sound like a goddamn saint."

"That's what elegies do. Everybody knows it's bullshit." He paused and looked at the surrounding cubicles and the nearby activity. "We need to talk."

Bob picked up on the request for privacy. "Uh, yeah. Come on."

He rose and led the way to an unused office. Once inside with the door securely closed, Scanlon said, "I want you to do something for me. You said the guy sent you the letters because of your column."

"Well, I'm not sure that's what happened…"

"I know, I know. But you're probably right. People know you; they see your picture in the paper every day. You're on TV. And there's the kind of column you write…"

"What's that mean?"

"Nothing. Forget it. Just a hunch. I want you to write a special column about Biggers' death. Drop a subtle hint that you could be contacted if, you know, anybody wanted to tell you anything. Like, offer to be a pipeline."

"You want the robber to send me another letter?"

"We're not talking about a fucking robber, Bob. Actually, I'm not even sure I know what I am talking about. It's routine cop stuff. If the guy wrote you once, maybe he'll write again."

"And if he does?"

"If he does we'll know a lot more about what's going on even if the message is only four words long."

"Tomorrow's column?"

"No. Write it first and let me see it. I'll let you know when to print it. Just comment on the case, don't mention the letters or give out any of the facts. No gun. Work it in that you're interested in the case. Suggest that you'd like input from readers, thoughts, or comments. Be a little vague. Maybe the guy will write again, he may slip up, say something he shouldn't and give us a lead as to what he's up to."

Bob sighed. "I hate to encourage my readers to write. I could end up with enough mail to give the mailman a hernia hauling the stuff in."

"I knew I could count on you."

"Only because I'm afraid you'll sic the IRS people on my ass if I don't cooperate."

"You don't really think the Bureau would do that, do you?"

"The hell I don't. Everybody knows you guys have no scruples."

Scanlon shook his head. "I'm glad Mr. Hoover isn't alive to hear such talk. It would break the poor man's heart."

"Hoover didn't have a heart."

"I know." He moved to the door. "I think we're going to become close pals, Bob. Real close."

Scanlon left Bob alone with his thoughts and they were numerous, indeed. What happened to the robbery theory? Who would write if it weren't the robber? What did he think the writer would write about? A confession? An apology? Why would anybody write at all? How would it help the murderer?

And what was that crack about being pals? He surely didn't mean socially. Cops always hang out with other cops so they can swap tales of derring-do and share tips on how to fake a back injury and get early disability retirement. The last guy cops want hanging around is a reporter looking for his next big story.

As a general rule, Bob didn't hang out with cops of any kind on the grounds that one never knew what they were thinking. Besides, he was a longtime admirer of the Rastafarians and frequently partook of their sacraments in order to commune with the spirits of Haile Selassie and Bob Marley and most cops prefer the company of boozers to tokers. In any event, cops and Bob didn't mix well so he wasn't enthused about teaming up with Jim (Dick Tracy) Scanlon.

When the cranial activity slowed a bit Bob reflected further on Scanlon's odd remark. There was obviously a lot more to Biggers' death than met the eye. He'd snapped sharply when Bob referred to the robber after Scanlon had abandoned that theory. Clearly, the agent was going in a different direction but what direction was that?

Bob gave up and went back to his cubicle and commenced writing the column requested.

CHAPTER FOUR

Bob finished Scanlon's column but never got the chance to use it since another senator turned up dead with a small hole in the back of his head for a change. The victim was Sen. Pat Goniff (R-AZ), a man of low moral fiber and totally lacking in integrity. He was such an untrustworthy schemer that even the lobbyists refused to bribe him, as the crooked bastard would vote against them because a rival had paid him more—and then keep their money in the bargain.

It seems the millionaire senator was on his way to visit his aged father in the County Poor House to have him sign documents that would strip the old-timer of his last possessions when some Good Samaritan shot him to death with a small-caliber gun. While one dead senator was a catastrophe, two dead senators were simply one too many and sure to alarm other senators who would rightly fear that there was some sort of irregularity going on that could affect their own well-being.

So Goniff's death threw everybody who knew the details into a wild panic that would have spread nationwide in hours, but almost no one knew the details because the feds swooped in and spirited the corpse away before it had even cooled off. The few who did know were hauled into backrooms and told to shut the hell up or the I.R.S. would audit them all the way back to childhood. Not a single person broke his vow of silence in what was a fitting tribute to the respect Americans have for the tax collector.

The senator's corpse was trucked off to the government's secret morgue just outside Fort Dix where the victims of federal malfeasance are stashed until the heat wears off. Some claim Judge Crater is there along with Amelia Earhart, Jimmy Hoffa, and Ambrose Bierce among others.

At a press conference officials claimed the senator had fallen chest first against a jockey lawn statue and broken his heart. Of course, those who knew the man were suspicious, as he was known to have a heart of stone that couldn't be broken in a lapidary's rock crushing machine but the feds held firm.

Anyway, the gendarmes went nuts. Top secret memos zipped back and forth across the country, search parties were organized, vacations cancelled, recruiting stepped up, Homeland Security alerted, bulletins posted as all stops were pulled to find the murderer before he could strike again.

What made this all so hard to pull off is that it had to be done in strict secrecy in order to avoid anything so dangerous as giving the public the truth. People might panic, the shock could snap minds, precedents might be set so the public would demand the truth on other matters and who knows where all this could lead?

Of course, Bob was among the uninformed, as well. There'd been no new letters after the first two and he hadn't talked to Scanlon for three days. That was remedied when he heard a tapping behind him. He turned as Scanlon spoke.

"Just passing. Any news?"

Bob shook his head. "Not a new, as Horace Greeley might put it."

"Hmm."

"You want to see your column?"

"Uh, no. We may not use it. I'm working on a new angle."

"It's Goniff, isn't it?"

"What is?"

"The new angle. It wasn't an accident, was it?"

"What have you heard?"

"That a lawn jockey killed him. Was the lawn jockey white or black?"

"Why?"

"I want to see if there was a racial angle."

Scanlon broke into a broad smile and shook his head. "You're a cagey bastard, Bob," he said. He looked left and right and leaned in. "This conversation is officially restricted. It's a major goddamn felony to repeat it. Got that?"

"Got it."

"It's Biggers again. Same MO. Same gun. No clues. Nothing taken."

"Jesus Christ!"

Scanlon nodded. "It's all top secret. We don't know what's going on but it's beginning to look like some sort of terrorism. Maybe Al Qaeda. Or some splinter group, local cells, freelancers…"

"There are freelance terrorists?"

"Sure. Remember those guys in Florida? They planned to blow up the Sears Tower in Chicago…"

"What? Those guys were no threat. They lived in Florida; they didn't even have bus fare to Chicago."

"They were making plans. People heard 'em."

"Then why did you let them go?"

"We didn't. They're going to trial."

"You're kidding!"

Scanlon ignored him. "It looks like Al Qaeda."

"It's a guess then?"

"An educated guess."

Through all this Bob kept his cool even while his heart leapt in his chest and his mind raced so fast he could smell traces of mental smoke as the words story of the century bounced around in his head like balls in a pinball game. He wanted to jump up and rush through the city room shouting, "Stop the presses! Stop the presses!" but he resisted the urge because he knew Scanlon would ship his ass to Guantanamo as an enemy combatant in a trice.

"So, uh, when do you think we could print the story?"

Scanlon straightened up. "Maybe never. I'll let you know."

He left and Bob clenched his fists and gritted his teeth and had to grab a desk to keep from sprinting to Pete's office with his scoop on the story of the century that could well produce Pulitzers for everybody. Oh, the humanity of it!

A week went by that saw the burial of the erstwhile senator from the National Cathedral in what was a reprise of Biggers' funeral with new cast members. This time the president didn't show up because Goniff's death had been declared an accident and it wasn't as dramatic as Biggers' sensational murder. Still, it was a moving experience with much grandeur and finery but the elegy clearly wasn't written in a country churchyard.

Sen. August Schwank, a boozy old man who'd been around so long people often hung their coats on him, made a windy speech on the deceased's life and accomplishments, but he went astray when he set out to enumerate his virtues.

"…me just list some of Pat's virtues here. Pat was above all else an honest man…" a chorus of groans from fifty lobbyists who'd come to gloat "…a man who was a true patriot…" a large American flag slipped on the wall and hung askew "…a God-fearing man…" a sea of heads swiveled on craning necks as everyone looked for falling statuary or other signs of Divine displeasure and the vicar winced noticeably. At last even Schwank saw that it was a lost cause and he trailed off in a series of grunts and monosyllables and finally proposed a toast and held his hand aloft until he realized nobody held a glass. Even the senator's corpse was so embarrassed by the whole affair that several witnesses claim they saw it blush.

Bob had come solo because Colleen was in L.A. for a fashion event and nobody else would go with him. He wasn't sure if this was an affront to him or if it merely reflected the little regard most people have for funerals as entertainment.

In any case, he ran into Ted Grinchy, an ex-congressman from Alabama. Ted was a devious guy widely known as a hypocrite for preaching family values while he was on his third marriage and umpteenth affair. The man had broken every Commandment except murder and regarded the Seven

Deadly Sins as words to live by. He'd been kicked out of Congress by an enraged electorate, threatened with tarring and feathering, and exiled forever from the state of Alabama. The Supreme Court later ruled Alabama couldn't exile him, but said that tarring and feathering would be okay.

"Bob, 'ol buddy!" Grinchy said. Small clumps of tar were still tangled in his hair and an overall odor of hot tar emanated from his person.

Bob put on the usual feigned smile appropriate for the occasion and said, "Hey, Ted. I haven't seen you since, well, uh, since they rode you out of town on a rail."

"Yeah, but that was a case of mistaken identity. The mob was after a different asshole. I just happened to look like the asshole they were after, is all."

"Well, sure, that could happen to anybody. What are you up to now?"

"Lobbyist. I signed on with the tobacco guys. I'm working on a new bill to allow candy cigarettes in school lunch boxes. I've already signed up fourteen senators and sixty House guys and it only cost us two million bucks."

"But if you give kids candy cigarettes isn't there a chance they'll want to smoke real cigarettes later?"

"Christ, I hope so. If they don't I'll be out of a goddamn job."

"Yeah, that makes sense."

"Say, what's with Biggers and Goniff?"

"Nothing. Why? Did you hear something?"

"No. Nobody knows anything. It just looks funny, like the fuckers are keeping a lid on it."

"It beats me. I don't know any more than you do. The cops hardly ever tell me what they're thinking."

"You buy that lawn jockey story?"

"Who knows? It could happen. You know how it holds its arm out for the reins? Well, if you tripped and fell forward that arm could hit your heart and that might break it."

"Maybe. I still think it looks funny."

"Say, listen, I've got to run here. I'm due back at the office by one-thirty."

"Give my bill a mention in your column. I'll send some free samples for your kids."

"You're all heart, Ted."

Bob moved off in a blue funk brought on by exposure to one of the Ted Grinchys of the world. As he reached his car he looked back and said aloud, "The goddamn tar wasn't hot enough, Ted."

For the next four weeks nothing happened, as far as the general public knew. The feds were so thorough in burying the truth along with the senator's corpse that his encounter with the lawn jockey was regarded as true and nobody even questioned it a month later. It was a fait accompli.

But the feds were busy. Dragnets quietly made a mockery of the arguments against racial profiling by hauling in Arabic-looking guys by the score even though almost all of them were citizens and real patriots. Hundreds were seized in Dearborn, Michigan, alone because there are a half-million Arab-Americans in that town and it's easier to round them up there.

Work was started on expanding Guantanamo to hold 5,000 suspected enemy combatants — or innocent persons of interest, whichever the president chose to send there—and seminars on effective torture techniques were held to train torturers. All applicants for torture training were Republicans because they couldn't find any Democrats who would do such work even for Halliburton-style wages. It was all perfectly legal, of course, as the president had officially approved torture and even outsourced it to our allies who have even fewer scruples than we do.

There was an attempt to hire illegal Mexicans as torturers because everybody knows they'll do a lot of jobs Americans refuse to do, but Mexicans have too much class and pride and they refused even when the feds offered them free green cards. There is now a movement afoot to give citizenship to all who refused because those are just the sort of real Americans we want in our country.

Again, this was all off-stage activity. No publicity, no press conferences. As far as the people knew there was no emergency. Biggers had been killed in a robbery, Goniff was felled by a statue. New senators had been appointed by their respective governors and were already hard at work establishing useful connections with lobbyists and learning how to abuse earmarks and all was right with the world.

Still, nothing was accomplished in spite of all the covert activity. Interest waned with the public, congressional members plundered on, deals were made in a business as usual world and the murders of two U.S. senators went unsolved. It is quite possible that things would have continued in this vein indefinitely if it weren't for the third senator's untimely demise.

This one was hard to cover up as Sen. Max Abbott had gone back to his home state to attend a banquet in his honor and was shot dead in the parking lot of a joint featuring reviews with all-naked ladies. His aides hastily pointed out that he was there on a fact-finding mission to investigate abuses in the strippers' industry but it was all academic because of the hole in the man's forehead. The senator would enjoy no more lap dances.

It was hard to cover up as half-a-dozen reporters from the Journal were holding a seminar there titled Morality in Journalism and they hit the parking lot almost as soon as the senator did. Four or five half-naked strippers joined the reporters and blocked the view of some observers, a fact that may explain why few of the witnesses could remember much about the actual crime.

Fortunately, several female onlookers managed to get cell phone pictures of the fallen senator and the telltale hole was shown in close-up. There would be no fantastic tales of lawn jockeys this time; the senator had been shot dead and everybody knew it—or at least they did once the reporters regained their wits and raced off shouting, "Stop the presses! Stop the presses!" They had the whole thing on the Internet within the hour and the a.m. edition all over town by dawn. Even Scanlon wasn't quick enough to quash the story and that meant he'd have to fall back on the truth.

Bob wasn't waiting for Scanlon this time. He heard the story on The Today Show as he was just sitting down to a waffle swimming in syrup and a mug of arabica coffee that scented the air with so fragrant an aroma as would make Pavlov salivate. He forked up a generous bite of waffle, swished it around in the syrup, and raised it mouth ward when Sen. Abbott's slain form appeared on the screen. It took a second or two for Bob to realize what he saw because the picture showed the forms of the half-naked girls in the background and, naturally, that was the first thing that caught his eye.

Once focused, he dropped the fork, knocked over the coffee mug, snatched up his briefcase at the door and was on the freeway before all the coffee had run off onto the floor. He sped from the parking garage to the lobby and into an elevator already full when he arrived. Moments later he barged into the editor's office and raised his hand and started to shout, "Stop the presses!"

But the magic of the moment was lost when Pete cut him off. "I already stopped the presses!"

"What? Shit!"

"You heard about Abbott?"

"The gloves are off, Pete. No more dancing around with Scanlon and his secrecy crap. It's Pulitzer time! We lay the whole story out, the letters, the real story on Goniff, tie 'em all together…!"

"And play up those letters! You're the contact man. Whatever is going on out there, you've got an inside track…!"

"It looks like terrorists, it really does. Somebody's assassinating our fucking political leaders. But who?"

"Israel?"

"Israel? Why would they want to kill our political

leaders?"

Pete shrugged. "I don't know but they're the experts at assassinations. The Mossad knocks off two or three Arab politicians or generals every week. One of 'em even dresses in drag for dramatic effect."

"Well, I'm pretty sure it's not Israel."

"Then it's Al Qaeda. That's their new plan. They'll kill off the entire Senate one at a time and throw the country into disarray."

"That would be a redundant plan. The country was already in disarray before all this crap happened. Even so, I think you're right and so does Scanlon. The feds gave up on the robbery theory right from the start and that only leaves those terrorist pricks as suspects."

Pete took Bob by the arm and turned him toward the door. "So, write! Fill up that screen. No holds barred!"

Although actually scooped by the Journal story, Bob was privy to stuff nobody else had, critical facts that colored everything. It would all be there in the Sentinel the next day, the actual wording of the letters and the revelation that Goniff didn't run afoul of a lawn jockey but was another victim of unknown assassins.

He also called on Homeland Security to rally its forces and urged readers to be on the alert for suspicious guys doing bizarre things, but this last wasn't effective, as there are too many such characters to keep track of and it could prove embarrassing. For example, one would have to begin with Congress itself and that would be awkward.

Bob typed the last words and leaned back with a soft smile on his mug as Pulitzers danced in his head when his cell phone broke his reverie. He took it from his pocket, flipped it open, and checked the caller's number.

"Fuck you, Scanlon," he said. He flipped the phone shut, leaned back, and closed his eyes.

CHAPTER FIVE

Bob's story created a sensation. Even average Americans could see that all was not kosher when three U.S. senators are shot dead in the space of a few weeks. A serial killer scenario was held by people who thought we should be looking for some guys in an old car with a hole cut in the trunk for sniper fire but those guys were in jail already. A few even thought the shootings were coincidental and that the killings would stop after the third one. Some of the most enlightened posited the theory that the feds themselves were shooting senators, a scenario not as loony as one might think.

But everybody else knew better including the feds. Director Slinker called a meeting of his top aides to address the new direction the case had taken. As the lead agent on the case, Scanlon was in the unenviable position of being the fall guy, the bozo who takes the rap to spare the big guys any responsibility or embarrassment.

All this was taken directly from the F.B.I. Official Manual, which specifically declares in Provision B #6 that, "...every Bureau operation requires that a particular Agent be specified as the fall guy who will be blamed for whatever goes wrong. Said Agent will be required to take one for the team, to spare the Bureau criticism that may redound to its harm or interfere with the careers of the Director, et al. In other words, the fall guy must fall on his sword and the Director will hold it for him."

Scanlon acted accordingly and carefully prepared his report to save his own skin without violating Provision B #6. He faced the stern visages of his superiors with an assured air of confidence that he was without stain in this matter and had done all the right things from day one. Still, he carefully scanned the room to see if there might be the odd sword lying around.

Director Slinker eyed him suspiciously. "You said it was a robbery, Scanlon," he said.

Actually, of course, Slinker was the one who said that but Scanlon wisely refrained from correcting him. "Yes, sir, but you insisted it was something much more than a mere robbery and you were obviously right."

An approving murmur rose from the aides and their nodding heads resembled a lot of Bobblehead dolls on dashboards. Slinker frowned.

"So we followed your advice, sir, and focused on the terrorist theory," Scanlon went on, "and the latest developments indicate that this theory is most likely true and that foreign agents have launched an all-out attack on the United States by assassinating our political leaders."

More murmurs and head bobbing. Slinker shifted his bulk and cleared his throat and everybody leaned forward to receive his benediction or curse, whichever it turned out to be.

"It is not a theory," he rumbled, "it is a proven fact. Our agents arrested an Arab man in Dearborn, Michigan, by the name of Assad Mohammad. He had cleverly disguised himself as a holy man and actually lived in a mosque to further deceive us. We sent him to Egypt where he was questioned by Egyptian authorities and he readily confessed his crimes."

Aides exchanged glances of approval and nodded some more.

"We know the people committing these vile murders are from Baghdad and are Sunni or Shiite Muslims. We aren't positive which it is since all of these guys look alike but our informant is certain that they're one or the other."

Murmurs and bobbing.

"We've already located several cells where these terrorists met and planned their attacks. Last night our agents raided a dozen coffee houses, two mosques, sixteen 7-Elevens, ten gas stations, and arrested 240 Arabs—I mean, persons of interest. They're on their way to Cuba as we speak and we should have full confessions by the weekend at the latest."

The aides nodded vigorously, shook their fists, elbowed each other, and generally expressed their approval.

"I've also ordered bodyguards for every senator; they'll have protection 24/7 until the killers are caught. The Secret Service is doubling security around the White House and the Capitol building and the local police will increase street patrols on the lookout for any Arabs…or, uh, persons of interest. We're taking people from the airports to beef up security elsewhere as almost all senators fly in private jets furnished them for free by corporate America and never go near commercial airlines."

"But, sir," Scanlon said, in a sudden burst of reason, "what if terrorists do attack planes? Won't that put private citizens at greater risk?"

A hush fell over the room, jaws dropped, eyebrows shot up, fearful glances flew in all directions. Slinker leaned back haughtily and glared down his nose at Scanlon who visibly shrank into his suit until it hung limply on him like a coat on a scarecrow.

"Save private citizens instead of U.S. senators?" He scowled fiercely and swung his gaze past his shocked aides and then broke out in laughter at the very idea and every sycophant in the room, which is to say everybody, broke out in a chorus of hearty laughter and gave each other high fives and had a grand time at poor Scanlon's expense as he grinned sheepishly and squeezed even deeper into his suit.

The Director regained control and said, "By God, Scanlon, that was a good one. Citizens before senators. Heh, heh. You've got a sense of humor there, Jim. Isn't that right, boys?"

Slinker left still chuckling and every man jack of them followed his example and chuckled all the way down the hall before they could risk stopping. Scanlon stood alone in the empty room, the grin still frozen on his face, as he watched the rest of his life pass before his eyes.

As for the senators, they reacted like the draft dodgers most of them are and loudly brayed that they are U.S. senators and their safety must be assured if the country was to be saved, etc. Few of them saw the irony in this because they were themselves a greater threat to the nation than any number of terrorists and that culling the Senate might very well end with an improved body, one whose members might even read the Constitution from time to time.

The president, unfortunately, had scheduled a vacation weeks before these events took place and was unable to change his plans because the tickets and prepaid reservations were not refundable. Many thought he should stay anyway because of the emergency, but it had been almost four months since his last vacation and, since he was the decider, he decided to take the vacation.

"Hey, it's not like I won't be in touch," he said in the Rose Garden, his trademark smirk playing about his mouth. "If there's any deciding to do I can be reached 7/24 at, uh, you know, just call the White House and they know where I am. So you all, uh, you have a nice vacation, too, when, uh, if you get a vacation, because I understand vacations, and I know some people don't get one and I intend to do something about that, too, just as soon as I get back. Heh, heh.'"

Sporadic applause accompanied by much eye rolling and open sneering followed his disappearing form as he ducked into the White House. While many were dismayed that the president would vacation under the circumstances, others were glad he was out of the way and less likely to bomb Iran or give new tax cuts to the rich while the rest of us were distracted by the latest savage terrorist attack on the United States.

Of course, the story flew across the nation literally at the speed of light or, on this occasion, at the speed of electronic signals via TV, radio, and the 'Net. Pundits had a field day laying blame and offering opinions that corresponded with their own particular biases and prejudices. Right wing radio talk show hosts filled the airwaves with nonsense and buncombe and urged the arrest of everybody in sight while more reasoned voices of the liberal media offered sage advice and encouraged a responsible approach.

Several senators who had long opposed the Second Amendment began carrying guns for protection, which the Bill of Rights specifically said ''...shall not be infringed.'' Of course, the vice-president wasn't allowed to have a gun because of that thing in Texas. Everyone was afraid the fool would shoot another guy in the face and he well might have, as we all know the veep's not a straight shooter.

It was a dubious deal, anyway, because the first day senators showed up carrying guns Bailey (R-UT) shot Slivovitz (R-MS) in the spleen while they were practicing their quick draw in the Senate cloakroom. The incident proved more serious than at first thought. It seems the bullet had damaged the organ and severely limited the future production of spleen. For most this wouldn't be a concern but Slivovitz was famous for venting his spleen on just about everybody and being without excess spleen changed his whole personality.

He turned into a nice guy with humanitarian instincts, a combination that assured disaster for a Republican in a party where these qualities were not only unknown but much decried. A month later he was caught on tape giving money to a homeless person on the street and Majority Leader Hoskins stripped him of his Chairmanship of the Earmarks Committee and the poor wretch's career was effectively ended.

For his part, Bob found himself basking in an international spotlight when it was learned he'd been in touch with the killer. Every paper in America snatched up his column and it went worldwide as the news spread that the nation was under a fresh attack by international terrorists. Requests for interviews poured into the Sentinel's city room by the thousands, the phones literally never stopped ringing.

In a word, Bob's world had morphed into something unique, edgy, strange, and even a little scary. While he didn't know it then it was a world he would continue to inhabit for the rest of his life.

CHAPTER SIX

Of course, Bob didn't have all that much to tell people other than what he'd already written. Aside from the two brief letters he'd learned nothing more about the matter. He decided to go underground for everybody's sake. His editor agreed.

"Good idea," Pete said. "This place is bedlam. If we tell 'em you're in France or someplace maybe they'll give us a little slack."

"I was thinking maybe a little closer to home. Like home."

"Okay, so go. And don't come back until you hear from me. Don't answer your phone or the door. Make like you're Salmon Rushdie hiding out in Mecca."

"I'm on my way."

Bob grabbed his laptop and briefcase and rode the freight elevator down to the loading dock, ducked out to the parking lot, and sped homeward like a tipsy Irishman fleeing a banshee. He never made home, though. As he turned down his street he saw a traffic jam ahead with media trucks, huge satellite dishes, cops everywhere, people massed in front of his condo building, and no chance of getting into his place in one piece. He turned into a driveway, backed out, and quietly drove off.

He turned the corner, pulled to the curb, and punched in numbers on his phone. Colleen answered.

"Hi, it's me."

"Christ, where are you? Everybody's looking for

you. A guy offered me a thousand bucks if I'd tell him where to find you."

"I'll give you two grand if you don't. Listen, I'm in hiding but I need a place to hide. I went home but there's a goddamn media army bivouacked in front of my condo. Can I stay with you?"

"Are you asking to move in with me?"

"No."

"Good. Ben Franklin said fish and relatives stink in three days. I'll give you three days."

"I need a key."

"Didn't I give you a key?"

"You know you didn't."

"Don't say it like that. You never gave me a key to your place."

"Only because I'm afraid you might use it."

Colleen sighed and laughed softly. "I'll meet you at my place in thirty minutes."

"You're a doll."

Bob flipped his phone shut and sat musing for a few minutes while he tried to sort things out. He finally gave up and drove off to what he hoped would be a safe house to thwart his pursuers. If Rushdie could pull it off for eighteen years, Bob figured he could hold out over a long weekend.

Colleen was prompt as promised and there were no media trucks or satellite dishes lining the street where she lived. Bob looked both ways and emerged from some shrubbery alongside the building to meet her at the door.

Colleen shivered in the heat and said, "I can't believe how goddamn jumpy I am!"

"Yeah, it's kind of eerie, isn't it? Like the whole world's gone nuts."

Bob opened the door and they entered the foyer where Colleen unlocked the lobby door. She stopped for her mail and minutes later they were in her apartment eight floors above media types and senator assassins. Bob took a deep breath and emitted a sigh that befitted such an occasion.

"Whew! I'm exhausted! I feel like I've just spent eight hours on a high-wire act over Niagara Falls."

"Small wonder. I'm exhausted too and I'm not even part of the act."

Bob reached out and pulled her to him. "Hey, partner, you're not only part of the act but you're an accomplice for hiding me out. If the terrorists come after me they'll get you, too."

She pulled away. "The terrorists are after you?"

Bob laughed what he hoped was a reassuring laugh and said, "The terrorists aren't after me. I'm their pipeline. Besides, so far they only shoot senators. I'm safe as long as I don't stand too close to any senators."

"Then I'm safe if I don't stand too close to you?"

"Uh, yeah, I guess you could say that."

Colleen took a wary step back. "I'll make us some lunch. You can wait here."

She left and Bob moved to a coffee table, lifted the lid from a small case thereon, and took out a fat hand-rolled joint that would have won the approval of Bob Marley himself. He held it up and inhaled its delicate aroma, smiled in anticipation of pending sensuous delights, and followed Colleen into the kitchen.

She looked up and raised a cautionary hand. "Not too close!"

Bob grinned and held up the joint. "I brought protection. Nothing bad ever happens if one is nicely stoned."

"Is that true?"

"No, I just made it up."

Colleen laughed and so did he. She turned away to make the lunch while he put flame to joint and inhaled deeply the magical smoke of the noble marijuana bush. She assembled a light lunch of extra-sharp cheddar cheese, cold salmon, thick chunks of sourdough rye bread, and sweet midget pickles on the side. They shared the joint as she worked and demonstrated Newton's second law of thermodynamics and entropy when said joint was reduced to roach status.

Though both drank little alcohol, they did enjoy wine with food and each kept assorted wines on hand for the table. A nice Merlot served the purpose on this occasion and when mixed with cheese, salmon, good bread, sweet pickles, and a little high-grade pot it proved to be a meal fit for them. They grew more relaxed and at ease with every bite, sip, and inhalation until the events of the day receded from memory.

Bread crumbs on the table top, wedge of cheese and knife on a plate, wine glasses half empty, a still life waiting for an artist's brush. Neither spoke for a full minute.

"A memorable meal."

"Yes."

"Know what? I haven't even got a toothbrush."

"Hmm. Maybe I could sneak into your place and

get your stuff."

"But you don't have a key."

"Then you won't brush your teeth for seventy-two hours."

"Would that bother you?"

"Not at all because you won't be staying here."

"Oh. Okay, I'll give you the key but promise you won't look at all my stuff."

"Don't be silly, of course I'll look. I'll check every drawer, look under the sink, read your e-mail…"

"Oh! I feel so violated!"

Colleen rose and began putting things away. "Let's get some air on the balcony." She filled Bob's glass. "Take your wine with you."

Bob carefully carried his brimming glass with him as Colleen wiped the crumbs up and put knife and plates in the dishwasher. She added wine to her glass and started for the balcony.

While not large the balcony provided a panoramic view of the city sprawled out before them. It was a static scene yet constantly changing with the time of day or night and the shifting of the light. Even sounds from the streets far below seemed to affect the view, or at least add another dimension to it.

They sat in parallel recliners with a small table between them. Pretty red and white flowers in planters stood at one end of the balcony and a pink plastic flamingo leaned tipsily against the wall at the other end in an obeisance to kitsch art.

As is often the case with friends of long standing, neither felt the need to talk. Somehow mere proximity could not only make words superfluous but might even interfere with real communication. At other times, though, words are crucial to understanding and this was one of those times.

Colleen started it. "So."

"Hmm?"

"Where do you see yourself in thirty days?"

"Forgotten. They'll catch the terrorists, everybody will confess, they'll hang the bastards, and my fifteen minutes will be over."

"What if they don't catch them? What if more senators are killed?"

Bob frowned as he came back to the real world. "I don't know. Maybe we should surrender. Pay 'em off like we did the Barbary Coast pirates in 1805."

"Seriously, where will all this end?"

Bob sat up. "Shit, I guess the war on terrorism will just go on. How do you win a war when you don't even know who the enemy is? We may eventually run out of senators. The Director of Homeland Security will be a lifetime job with a pension and benefits, and America will turn into a giant Baghdad."

It was a pleasantly warm evening but Colleen shivered again. "Jesus Christ, that's the gloomiest thing I ever heard!"

"Tell it to those poor bastards in Baghdad. They've lived with it for five years."

"Maybe it isn't terrorists," Colleen said hopefully.

"Nothing else makes any sense."

"Shit."

"Yeah."

Later that evening Colleen made the trip to Bob's digs to retrieve his gear without incident. The media still filled the street with people and equipment and dozens of suspicious onlookers eyed her closely on her way in and as she left with a small overnight bag but none recognized her. She helped assure her anonymity by wearing a floppy straw hat that concealed her blonde hair and oversized dark glasses which acted as a virtual mask in a disguise that might have deceived a close relative.

She did not, it should be noted, look through Bob's stuff as such an act would be infra dig for any person with class, a quality Colleen possessed in spades.

Once outfitted with clean clothes and toilet articles, Bob stayed the allotted three days and never once left the apartment. The news raged in every sort of media available, cries rang out on all sides demanding action, interview requests turned into demands as tension and passion rose.

Even the feds wanted to talk to him. Scanlon besieged Pete with demands that Bob come forth but the editor wasn't easily swayed with threats and he stoutly refused to reveal his location. Colleen came and went and nobody ever thought that she might be harboring Bob, as their relationship had always been low key with many not knowing there was any relationship at all.

All in all, his sojourn served him well. After three days he felt rested and fit again and ready to reengage the enemy in his ongoing fight for liberty and justice.

In brief, life was good again even if only temporarily.

CHAPTER SEVEN

Bob reached the Sentinel building at mid-morning in hopes of avoiding the media still camped in the street and even then he only succeeded by ducking around back and entering through a little used door to the boiler room. The engineer gave him a cheery salute as he hurried to the freight elevator.

When he finally reached the office the first person he ran into was a pissed-off Scanlon who was busy upbraiding the editor for high crimes and misdemeanors for not producing Bob on request.

"Where the hell have you been?" he demanded.

"Why? Were you looking for me?"

"You know damn well you're supposed to stay in touch with the Bureau."

"Nobody told me that."

"You shouldn't have to be told that. Wasn't it obvious?"

"Hey, I don't work for you guys." He pointed to Pete. "That's my boss. He said I could take some vacation time and I did. I don't have to run that by you."

Scanlon tried a new tack. "Look, Bob, the goddamn country is under attack. We don't know what the fuck is going on and you're the only man in America that's ever heard from these guys. That makes you a major player whether you like it or not. It isn't just me or the Bureau that needs you; it's the whole goddamn country. Remember, the president could declare you essential to national security and draft your ass under the War Powers Act."

"And send me to Gitmo? That would be really stupid."

Scanlon leaned in and spoke softly. "Are you the only guy in America who doesn't know that doing stupid things is our president's principal claim to fame?"

Bob recoiled in mock horror. "That's treason! You could be shot for saying that."

"Shot, hell!" Pete snorted. "He'd be a hero."

Scanlon shook his head. "I'd deny it, anyway."

Bob sighed. "Look, I don't want trouble. I'm as patriotic as the next guy and if I can help I will. I just don't like being hounded, that's all. Besides, there's nothing I can do unless they contact me again. I don't know any more than you do beyond that."

"Okay, forget all that. Let me put it another way. We need you. Please say you'll pitch in and help out until this thing is over."

Bob shrugged and offered his hand. "Deal. I promise I won't disappear again."

Scanlon took his proffered hand and said, "Good. Now, in your next column, I want you to make a direct appeal for them to contact you. Straight out. Don't be subtle. Just say you need to talk to someone, anyone, anywhere, anytime. A live person, if not in real time then virtually. Will you do that?"

Again, Bob looked to the editor and got the go sign.

"Yeah, I'll do that."

"And if they offer to meet you'll go?"

"Only if I get the Medal of Freedom. If the president can give those other assholes a medal he can give me one, too."

"Help us catch these pricks and you can have any goddamn medal you want."

"I want that one."

Now it was Scanlon's turn to say deal and he did. "Deal."

So it was that Bob was back in harness and in for the long haul. He had no idea exactly what that would entail but he would know soon enough.

He wrote Scanlon's column and it ran the next day but it drew a blank. There was a lot of response but it was all from readers remarking on his appeal for a reply. Scanlon, et al., weren't sure what the silence meant, whether the terrorists were suspicious or had just moved on. Some felt it might have been better if they hadn't made the appeal since the original silence wasn't as ominous as the one they'd provoked.

In any case, the hunt for terrorists surged ahead on all fronts. The president called from his secret vacation hideaway and ordered his ambassador-at-large, The Hon. Charles Finley, to go to the Middle East and meet with area leaders to seek their help in calling off their agents.

Many claim that Chuckie, a disreputable old fraud and the president's pal when they served in the Texas Air National Guard together, only got the job because he knew the truth about the president's service record in Alabama and could prove what he knew.

In other words, Chuckie knew the president had cut and run and was therefore subject to the death penalty, as desertion during a time of war is punishable by death. The president thought it might prove disquieting if he were shot dead by a firing squad so he bought off the opposition to spare the nation such a spectacle.

It was an opportunity lost; a timely firing squad would have spared the nation the entire Iraq war, saved countless lives, and a trillion dollars in hard cash. What a shame.

Anyway, Finley started at once for Cairo by way of Paris where he lingered for three days while his wife shopped. Next, he hastened to Rome where he met with the pope and accepted two nice Italian silk suits, a gift from the Pontiff. Then it was on to Athens for two days and finally to Cairo where he met with President Mubarak who distracted the old fool with a guided trip to Southern Egypt where countless others had been buried before Mubarak buried The Hon. Charles Finley next to them.

And so the weeks passed and no more senators died. Some hoped that Bin Laden had ordered his terrorists to stop and would soon sue for peace, but most felt it was the bodyguards that now accompanied every senator wherever he went. Would-be killers simply found opportunities reduced to zero but it was no victory for the government in the end.

That was made clear five weeks after Goniff was dispatched to hell's fiery furnaces when Rep. Andrew Snavely (R-TX) was found deader than a doornail with the hallmark hole in his head. The owner of numerous slum properties in Houston and a board member of the Houston Better Business Bureau, he had just evicted a single mom with three small children because she was a week late with her rent. He watched impassively as she struggled off down the street, a battered suitcase holding all her worldly goods. He went back into the apartment and nodded with satisfaction at a job well done.

That's where they found him, a surprised look on his mug, his briefcase empty, and eviction notices scattered around his fallen form. A group of neighbors stood in front of the building and everyone wore a wide smile. What could not have been much fun for Snavely had been the liveliest of events for those who knew him best.

But that wasn't the worst of it. Snavely was killed just before noon but his body wasn't found until 2:30 p.m. In the interim Rep. Henry Hacker, (R-KY), a member of the Ethics Committee and widely known as a liar and humbug who routinely sold out the country for personal gain, was en route to his own rendezvous with the Grim Reaper. He left his office in Louisville at 1:15p.m. for a meeting with some fellow crooks when a lone gunman stepped from a doorway and shot him dead. As the now defunct congressman crumpled to the pavement a large crow in a nearby tree cawed loudly.

Well, that pretty much did it. The country was in for it and everybody knew it. Denied their senatorial targets, the terrorists adopted a new strategy: if they couldn't shoot senators, they'd shoot House members instead. Nobody thought to give representatives bodyguards partly because there are 435 of them as opposed to 100 senators and cost became a factor.

All that changed now. Congressmen threatened to stay home if not given armed guards of their own and the nation rejoiced, a result that served as a warning that voters thought very little of their representatives and might even wish some of them dead. Two representatives actually resigned and forswore politics forever rather than run the risk of joining Biggers and company.

The president surfaced long enough to bray loudly about patriotism and family values and giving 110%, etc. He also reminded us that he'd said if we didn't stop them there, they'd come after us over here. The implication was that we deserved what we were getting and it served us right. By then it was 9:30 and he went to bed.

Twin funerals were held in the National Cathedral with the usual attendants and no expense was spared. There were two caskets, elegies, vicars, choirs, and sets of pallbearers with much fanfare equally divided between both guests of honor.

The president sent dual messages, which were read aloud by an aide who remarked that they had been written by the president himself, a fact that quickly became obvious since they were incoherent and garbled. Neither Snavely nor Hacker had any complaints about the proceedings so one might safely conclude both were pleased and felt they had their money's worth.

A pair of hearses was loaded up and left in two separate convoys, Snavely heading for a Catholic cemetery and Hacker for a crematorium as per the wishes of his family. They insisted it was either that or they would drive a stake into his heart to make sure the bastard was dead. Apparently, he hadn't valued his own family in spite of harping about family values over two decades.

The interim vicar of the National Cathedral, a Catholic priest subbing for his Protestant colleague, was delighted with the increase in business and silently hoped more pols would drop dead and add to his bottom line. In fact, on one occasion the vicar met with his assistant priests and a summer intern to discuss ways to squeeze more profit from their bonanza. When they weren't looking the Devil sneaked in and prodded the intern to suggest they might contact the terrorists and arrange for some sort of profit-sharing scheme.

The vicar beamed at the idea and the others followed suit until someone detected the faint odor of brimstone in the air and realized the Prince of Darkness was present. The outraged prebendaries sent him reeling with a broadside of prayers and imprecations and their souls were saved even if it was at the expense of the bottom line.

The vicar didn't inform the Vatican of this incident, as he knew the Pontiff would be sorely pissed with him for favoring principle over cash on the barrel head. After all, two millennia of tradition are not to be lightly ignored.

And so the number of dead politicians rose to five with the remaining 530 lawmakers reduced to nervous wrecks so scared that most stayed in their offices and refused to leave even for lunch or to answer roll call. As a result no crappy laws were passed during this period and the people were overjoyed, a situation that caused the pols to wax wroth at their inability to do mischief.

The boys holed up in Hoover's Palace were at

their wits' end. Two or three assassinated politicians were one thing but five was something else. While the average citizen wasn't too concerned for his own safety because the terrorists were only killing politicians, angry voices demanded action nevertheless if only for the sake of appearances.

Accordingly, things hummed at headquarters. Slinker ordered Scanlon to produce a viable plan by the next day or else. Scanlon quickly called a meeting of his own top aides and gave them the same ultimatum.

"Boys," he said earnestly, "we've got one day to come up with a plan. Either that or you can kiss your careers bye-bye. It's show time. We've got five murders and no clues. Any suggestions?"

MacTavish raised a hand. "Uh, I noticed that only Republicans have been killed, and, uh…"

"Say," Fisby said, "that's right! Does that mean…?"

"Jesus, the Democrats are killing the Republicans!" Chilson exclaimed.

"Holy shit!" several said in unison.

Scanlon was flabbergasted. "Jesus Christ! That could be it!"

All were stunned. It was so simple. Years of Republican brigandage, endless assaults on the Constitution, election rigging, Intelligent Design crap, stem cell vetoes, idiotic Kansas voters and more all proved too much for Democrats and they went berserk.

Ogilvy pursed his lips and stared thoughtfully at the names of the dead pols on a sheet of paper. After a moment he broke the silence. "I see something else that looks odd."

"Odd?" Scanlon said. "What's odd?"

"Well, it might not mean anything, but I noticed that all five of 'em are the biggest assholes in Congress."

Everybody stopped and ran through the names mentally and all quickly verified it.

"Jesus Christ!"

"It's true!"

"Oh, my God!"

Scanlon, mouth agape, collected himself by first closing his mouth and then speaking. "The biggest assholes. The most ignorant, greedy, hypocritical, bastards in Congress with voting records that would embarrass Boss Tweed. Each one with morals lower than sea level, unscrupulous, a demagogue, rogue, and charlatan, and the first targets of the assassins!"

"It's not terrorists at all!"

"It's the first break we've had!"

"That's right. Now we know who's killing our politicians and why."

"Wait a minute," Scanlon said. "There's something else here. Look at the list. Not only are they the worst assholes in Congress, but they were killed in the order of their degree of depravity!"

They applied more communal thought to the matter and saw that it was true. Biggers was easily the most depraved of the lot and the others fitted their assigned slots perfectly. All were astonished but that wasn't the last card to be played in this hand. Chilson played the ultimate card.

"A thought occurs to me," he said, to get their attention. All eyes swung his way. "We not only know who's killing our solons and why, but we also know how to catch the pricks." He paused for effect. "We'll know who the next target is if we can name the guy who's the sixth most evil asshole in Congress!"

It was a dramatic breakthrough, one that would be remembered by a large plaque prominently displayed in the Director's office to commemorate the moment. Through sheer brilliance alone the Bureau had solved what was probably the most important case in its history.

"So, all we have to do is watch number six until somebody tries to kill him!"

High fives were offered all around as they laughed and shook their fists and slapped backs and tripped off like the crowd at a Grateful Dead concert. Scanlon held a hand up to restore order.

"Wait a minute," he said, "how do we know who number six is?"

"That's easy, it's that asshole Bates. He was charged with breaking into lockers in the Senate gym."

"No, Snarles is our man. He introduced a bill to eliminate Social Security."

"I vote for Greasly. The son-of-a-bitch was caught on tape taking a hundred grand from a pharmaceutical lobbyist."

"How about Higgins…?"

"No, Cartwright..!"

"But…!"

It soon became apparent that they'd never agree on number six so they compromised and assigned shadows for the ten worst guys in the House with the thought that the next target was sure to be one on their list. The result was that the twenty most despicable assholes in the entire Congress had 24/7 protection while they served as bait.

It goes without saying that the potential targets were not informed of the new plan.

CHAPTER EIGHT

As it was the first real plan they'd had they chose to call it plan A. The pols were followed everywhere they went, many of them wearing body armor but not the same stuff we'd been sending the troops in Iraq. The solons got the latest technology; armor that was gossamer thin yet could stop a small artillery shell. It was the least we could do to protect our gallant legislators.

Naturally, the feds never bothered to tell the public that the Democrats and Republicans were engaged in internecine warfare to avoid revealing their plan, alerting the party hit men, and scaring the bejabbers out of the targets.

Another whole month sped by without further assassinations but public spirits went up little, as people were wary after the last hiatus that ended with Snavely and Hacker. Most folks held out for more time before committing themselves, maybe eight or ten weeks or so. It was a wise choice.

At the beginning of the fifth week sans new corpses people began to stir a bit. Politicians appeared here and there, often in fleeting glimpses as one ducked between parked cars or slipped furtively into a nearby doorway. Some even tried to disguise themselves as regular citizens but they didn't have enough substance to pull it off; it's easy to see through a politician if one just looks closely.

The legislative process had ground to a halt, as

we've seen. They couldn't round up a quorum if the pols refused to leave their offices. While this mattered little to the country, it mattered a great deal to the lobbyists. If no bills were being passed they'd start losing their enormous fees from corporate America and that was unacceptable.

The result was that pressure mounted on the authorities to arrest somebody, anybody. They'd had to release the two suspects arrested earlier, of course, but everybody knew they never counted from the beginning. Because Scanlon couldn't tell them about plan A, everybody thought the feds were doing nothing at all. The brilliant work of Scanlon's crew was going for naught and the Bureau just had to tough it out.

And suddenly none of this mattered. On a Tuesday afternoon in late July the rules changed, old actors were replaced with new ones, the survival of the nation was at risk, and the whole world was alarmed.

It had been a slow day. Bob was a column up for the week and thought about ducking out early but decided to stay and do the mail before he left. He went to the lounge for coffee and half of somebody's cruller and back to his cubicle to await the mail.

Fifteen minutes later the day's mail dropped onto his desk. There were two letters, one from a credit card company and the other with a return address in Las Vegas and a postmark from Scranton.

Bob's heart seemed to leap in his chest and turn somersaults. Another letter! The next installment. New killings? An explanation? A confession? Demands? A meeting? Should he call Scanlon? He stopped in mid-thought and said aloud, "Jesus Christ, open the letter!"

He shook the envelope and held it up to the light to make sure he wouldn't tear the letter when opening it and tore one end off. He took still another single sheet of stationery out, opened it, and read it aloud.

CASUS BELLI

> *Acting under the auspices of the Declaration of Independence, the American people hereby announce an armed insurrection against the abusive and oppressive Government of the United States of America.*
> *Accordingly, a State of War now exists between the Government and its people and will continue until such time as the Administration agrees to hear the peoples' complaints.   K*

Bob was stunned, astonished, confused, and scared all at once. Electrical charges shot around in his brain like bolts of lightning in Frankenstein's lab, thought waves crashed into each other, colored lights flashed and he watched it all as a disinterested spectator might watch fireworks in the night sky.

Slowly, almost as though in a slow motion film, Bob sipped his coffee, took a big bite of the cruller, and chewed thoughtfully. After a moment he stood and started for Pete's office, letter in one hand, coffee in the other, and a face shorn of expression.

He entered Pete's office, advanced to his desk, looked at him and said, "I know why."

"Why what?"

"Why they're killing politicians. It's tyrannicide."

"Tyrannicide?"

Bob nodded. "The killing of tyrants. The people are rebelling against the government of the United States." He handed him the letter.

Puzzled, Pete took the letter and read it. He looked up, shock on his face and in his voice. "Is this a fucking joke?"

Bob shrugged. "I think it's the real McCoy."

"A revolution?"

"That's what it says."

"But this isn't 1776, for Christ's sake! People can't go around attacking the goddamn government!"

"They already have. Those guys were killed because they were enemies of the State."

Pete picked up the phone and started punching in numbers. "Jesus Christ, we need the cops!"

"Can I yell stop the presses now?"

Scanlon showed up fifteen minutes later with a dozen agents who spread out in the city room and everywhere else as their leader practically ran into Pete's office. Pete didn't have time to speak; he just thrust the letter out in front of him and Scanlon snatched it roughly from his hand.

He read it in a single glance and then read it again slowly, one word at a time as though trying to commit it to memory, and then slowly lowered his hand.

"Holy fucking shit!" he said softly.

Bob nodded. "Tyrannicide. They're killing tyrants. It's a revolution."

"What?"

Pete nodded at Bob. "Okay, now."

Bob looked around the room and said quietly, "Stop the presses."

Those words reminded Scanlon that he was talking to reporters and he quickly reverted to form. "You can't publish this. It's top secret."

Pete shook his head. "Not this time, Dick Tracy. This stuff is news and that's what we do here."

Scanlon's face reddened and various veins on his head throbbed in time with some internal metronome measuring the intensity of his anger. "I'm ordering you not to publish classified information!"

Pete gestured to Bob. "Stop the presses, Bob."

Bob gave a snappy half-salute and started out.

Scanlon shouted to a nearby agent. "Stop that man!"

The agent made a grab for him but Bob feinted, pulled a neat veronica on him with a handy jacket on the back of a nearby chair, and whirled away with a move that would warm the cockles of Ernest Hemingway's heart. In a flash he sprinted by his would-be captor and out into the city room shouting, "Stop the presses! Stop the presses!"

Bob and Pete spent the night at F.B.I. headquarters as guests of the federal government. Both expected to be tortured and flown willy-nilly to Cairo for advanced-level torture at the hands of professionals who are certified at the trade, but a sudden burst of reason forced the feds to free them to avoid suppression of free speech charges that would only further encourage the rebels in their fight for better government.

So the Sentinel went ahead with the whole story from Biggers to Snavely and Hacker and the content of the letters including the latest one. One conjures up pictures of Paul Revere galloping westward, the redcoats hot on his heels. Headlines blared that the government was under siege by its own people, that a group of dissidents assassinated five senior pols and threatened to kill others if its demands were not met.

Surprisingly, while the news was shocking it was also received with less concern than one might have expected. For one thing, as we've seen, the rebels were judicious killers concentrated on assassinating politicians all of whom deserved their fate. It seems a great many Americans had already concluded that the country was in free fall insofar as sensible government was concerned and wondered what took so long for folks to start shooting.

Typical comments heard from widely disparate sources included comments such as, "It's about goddamn time!"

"I'd shoot the veep myself if I could!"

"It's the only way you'll ever get the bastards to give us universal health care."

"Good! They oughta hang the whole bunch of 'em!"

And so on.

Apparently, the timing couldn't have been better. The people were pissed after decades of growing arrogance and greed from their elected representatives. It was big business and corrupt politicians against everybody else in a scenario that grew ever worse for average citizens and ever more prosperous for the rich and it was now going to change even if it meant shooting every last one of the larcenous pricks.

As for Bob his star rocketed into the stratosphere. His column on the rebellion was reprinted in every newspaper on the planet and everyone wanted a piece of him. Evening news anchors called personally to appear on their shows, Larry King came and sat in the Sentinel's lobby and waited even after being told Bob was out of town and wouldn't be back for three days. Cronkite promised to come out of retirement to interview him, agents called to sign him to a book deal, Hollywood wanted the film rights, terrorists called to thank him for taking the heat off them and volunteered to kill a few of the senators themselves to help the cause.

In short, all that had gone before was as nothing compared to what was going down now and would continue in the future. All news took a back seat to the rebellion. Foreign journalists poured into the country and swarmed over the land in great hordes waving notebooks and mikes. Oddly enough, every single one of them wore a goofy grin on his mug that implied he was delighted to be a part of such an event and hoped they wouldn't run out of House members before the final curtain.

The president called an emergency Cabinet meeting for the next day to decide what position to take on the rebellion that would be most useful politically. They assembled at the White House and solemnly filed into the room and to their chairs, but two seats remained empty. It turned out that two Secretaries, one of Agriculture and the other of Interior, had phoned in their resignations the previous night and left the country. One or two of their colleagues gazed longingly on the empty seats and wished that they'd demonstrated the same foresight.

For politicians nationwide were scared witless. They all knew what scoundrels they were and feared just retribution at the hands of enraged patriots carrying pitchforks and M16s. In towns and cities and hamlets across America aldermen called in sick, council members tendered resignations, mayors headed for the border, judges shucked their robes and tried to blend in with average people. In an amusing aside four big-time pols dressed in drag were apprehended as they made a run for it, but it seems one of them was just on an outing.

Their fears were compounded by the fact that no one knew who their potential enemies were. How do you spot a rebel? Do you arrest everyone who displays a free spirit? Or a proud mien? Rebels all look alike, you can't tell one from another without a program. Your neighbor, friend, co-worker, preacher all may be covert freethinkers, iconoclasts, incipient insurrectionists looking for a chance to slit your throat to refresh that tree Jefferson mentioned.

All this tends to make a man edgy even as it delights the innocent who know they have nothing to fear and openly favor the rebels in their fight against tyranny and tyrants.

The president knew of the deserters but he wasn't really pissed because he felt a sort of kinship with them. Still, it did look bad and showed a lack of confidence and that part did piss him off.

"Boys," he said, including the women present and producing scowls on several of them, "you heard the news. America is under attack. We figure its Democrats. Probably gay people, a lot of lesbians and homos because they hate America. They want to take away our freedoms. So we need a plan."

He surveyed the audience with his customary smirk belying the seriousness of the moment and everyone stirred uneasily, not sure if he expected them to offer plans or if it was rhetorical. They were saved when a screen behind the president glided down and revealed the details of his plan to save America from the terrors of liberty and freedom.

He pointed at number one. "Now, the first thing is, we have all the governors call up the National Guard so we can protect…"

A tentative hand went up and the president frowned. The Secretary sitting on either side of Secretary of Defense Runnels edged his chair away to avoid possible political contamination by inappropriate proximity to a wrongdoer.

"Yes?" the president snapped.

"Uh, sir, uh, there aren't any National Guard units left to call up, sir. They're all in Iraq."

"What? All of 'em can't be in Iraq. What about my old outfit? The Texas Air National Guard? They're not in Iraq, are they?"

"Oh, no, sir," Runnels said, "everyone knows they never send the Texas Guard out of the country but all the rest are gone. It was the surge. We needed 50,000 new troops and we had to call up all of them. The only ones left now are really old guys and a lot of amputees…"

"So call 'em up! This is a bad time. People have to make sacrifices. Every man has to serve. We gotta fight 'em over here so we won't have to fight 'em over…!"

He stopped, looked befuddled, and tried to recover. "Heh, heh, it's like fool me once, fool me, uh, again…" He trailed off aimlessly and everyone squirmed.

He pointed at number two. "I signed an Executive Order this morning authorizing the construction of 200 Relocation Centers. They'll hold up to 500,000 persons of interest mostly in the western states like Idaho and Kansas." He pointed to Utah and South Dakota.

"I don't think we should call them Relocation Centers, sir," Runnels said. "I think the Supreme Court said they're illegal."

"They did, eh? Okay, let's call 'em camps. We could say we're sending people to camp. Camp is a good place."

Atty. General Schultz raised a hand and said, "We could reopen Manzanar in California. You could put five, six thousand right there."

The idea of reopening the camp where we illegally locked up Japanese-Americans in WWII wasn't smart for a lot of reasons but the president thought it was brilliant. He beamed at Schultz and said, "Now, that's thinking outside the box! We could reopen all those old WWII camps and save a fortune."

"But, sir, that's only a couple dozen camps," Secretary Schnorrer said. "Who will we get to build 175 more? Most Americans don't want to do that kind of work, you know."

"We'll use Mexicans," the president said. "Hell, the country's full of 'em and they work cheap, too. Few billion dollars and we'll have 'em ready for a national dragnet by spring. We'll arrest every Muslim in the country, make 'em stop wearing those funny hats and masks and…"

Again, Schnorrer risked a wrathful response. "Sir, the rebels are Americans. We can't arrest American citizens for no reason at all."

"The hell we can't!" Schultz rumbled. "What about Guantanamo? All we have to do is claim they're terrorists and bam! They get life without parole."

"Oh, wait," the president said, "I forgot. They're rebels. I thought we were after Arabs. Okay, so we round up rebels, we'll just call 'em terrorists because the Patriot Act says they don't have any rights then. How's that sound?"

"Good, sir!"

"Thank God for the Patriot Act!"

"Brilliant, Mr. President!"

He pointed to number three. "We're gonna bug everybody's phone, check their e-mail, put cameras on every street corner in America, run IRS audits on people we don't like…"

Runnels raised another tentative hand but the president stopped him short.

"I know, you're gonna say it's illegal but this is war. I'm using the War Powers Act. I can do anything I want if we're at war. The thing is we have to stop the terrorists before it's too late. They hate us for our freedoms. They want to take 'em away. It's my job as president to protect the American people. If we have to give up a few rights, why, at least the terrorists can't say they won."

Everybody nodded and gave thumbs up signs and made fists and generally indicated complete agreement like the true sycophants Cabinet members always are.

That's how they got there in the first place, of course.

The president smirked some more and pointed at number four. "We need intelligence. Everybody knows you have to be intelligent to win. That means we have to do whatever it takes to get information from the terrorists so we can know what they're thinking." He paused and assumed a guilty look. "That's why I'm giving the CIA new powers to, uh, interrogate suspects with, uh, new methods. Suppose there's a hidden H-bomb about to blow up New York City and Mohammad knows where it is. We have to make him talk. So we need experts who know how to do that."

By this time his audience was completely flabbergasted. No one spoke or even moved as he stopped. The president had just outlined a fascist government complete with camps and torture chambers and suggested we adopt 1984 as our model! This was too much even for Republican Conservatives, a group never noted for its interest in liberty and freedom. No one reacted and the president took this to mean they loved his plan when what he really got was a replay of the emperor's new clothes bit.

After a long awkward moment people stirred, the president rose and accepted congratulations from those nearest him while others on the fringe made hasty exits to avoid guilt by association raps.

Naturally, when his plan was made public there was a great clamor in the media and university campuses erupted with protesters, law professors cried foul, private citizens flooded everybody with e-mails, and Al Jazeera announced that the Muslims had won the war with the infidels and turned America into a state any mullah would be proud of.

And so the Second American Revolution got off to a flying start.

CHAPTER NINE

As the president's Cabinet meeting was in progress Bob met with Pete to follow up on the story that took the whole world by storm.

"…full time. This thing is going to be the biggest goddamn story since Lexington and Concord. Go wherever you have to, spare no expense, you're on it 24/7 until this is over."

Bob nodded. "Good. Maybe I can get K to meet with me. He must be the head guy since he does all the PR work."

"Sooner or later somebody has to meet with the government and he knows it. Their demands will have to be negotiated; there's no way we'll just turn the country over to a band of nobodies we've never even seen. See if you can arrange that meeting. Maybe act as a liaison between the feds and the rebels. Be the middleman."

"We tried that before, didn't we?"

"No. We never printed it. That was when they killed Goniff."

"Maybe I can scout around and see if I can scare up a rebel or two and get his input. If it's anonymous some of 'em might speak up."

"The feds will be on your ass to reveal every source you dig up, you know."

"Fuck 'em. They're the ones who got us in this mess to start with. Let 'em find their own persons of interest."

"Try reaching K again. Now that we know what's going on, maybe he'll be ready to take the next step. He has to get his message out and it looks like we're his first choice. He needs us."

Bob nodded. "Tomorrow's column." He didn't speak for a moment and then said, "We have a Gray Eminence on our hands, don't we?"

"What?"

"K. The man behind the scenes, a power broker we don't know. He pulls the strings, or knows who does, and things happen that he wants to happen."

"That sounds kind of scary."

"Depends on what things he wants to happen. God knows we've got a bunch of corrupt bastards in Congress; maybe we should purge the whole lot."

"Rebels always have a good cause for war. People only rebel when somebody's beaten the crap out of 'em for a long time."

"It does have familiar overtones, doesn't it?"

"Yeah. Seventy-six of 'em."

"Who would have thought it?"

Bob stood to leave and Pete said, "What about those media vultures? How are you going to handle all that crap?"

"Ignore it. No interviews, no speeches. Tell 'em the feds won't let me discuss the case."

Pete shook his head. "Good luck with that. You'll have a mob on your heels everywhere you go."

Bob looked out of the window at the van with the dish on its roof and left by the freight elevator in what became his preferred method of egress. He didn't park in the lot as lookouts were posted at the entrances.

Instead, he was able to slip alongside the building behind piled newsprint and drums of ink and reach a corner where a quick step or two put him in the rear of a pottery store where a thousand pots big and small were stored. From there he could reach the next street and walk two blocks down to a small lot where he'd parked.

He started for home and remembered the mob scene so he made a u-turn and headed back to Colleen's place.

They ate dinner in even though Colleen's place wasn't under siege because Bob feared being recognized and trampled to death in the rush if he went out in public. After dinner they shared a fat doobie while watching the news on TV and saw worldwide reports on America's startling revolution. It wasn't surprising, given America's performance in recent years, to learn that our neighbors all rooted for the rebels against the current Administration. Our nation's favorable ratings around the world were lower than Death Valley and it showed.

Bob frowned at the screen. "The bastards all hate us."

"I wonder why."

"Maybe they're right. Maybe the rebels should win and make 'em do the right thing for a change."

"They've got the right idea. They'll only get what they want at the point of a gun."

"So, whose side are we on?"

"Do you have to ask?"

"Hmm. Still, they're also assassins and that's not cool."

Colleen sipped her wine and said, "Personally, I've always thought Jefferson was a very wise man."

Bob looked at her. "That's what I like about you; you go right to the heart of a matter. Jefferson *was* a wise man and his tree analogy is right on. The fat, greedy, unpatriotic fuckers deserve what they get. They've sold the country out dozens of times, made Ali Baba's 40 thieves look like penny-ante crooks, and raised lying and corruption to new heights."

"What else is new?"

Bob sighed a mighty sigh. "It's true. Socrates could have heard the same stuff in any Athenian coffeehouse."

"They didn't have coffee in Athens then."

"Oh, yeah, that's right. Well, any wine shop. They all drank like sailors, you know."

Colleen put her glass down and snuggled close to him. "What do you think? We can go clubbing tonight and dance into the wee hours or stay home and watch a movie."

"We never go clubbing."

"I know. That's why we're going to watch a movie."

So they watched a movie and matters proceeded in the meantime.

The next day the Sentinel's headline shouted, "Gray Eminence Unveiled!" with Bob's column the featured source of the quote. The phrase was loaded with mystery and intrigue, cloaked figures behind closed doors, secret forces at work, suspense. The expression was perfect for K and his machinations, catchy and brief and sinister, and it caught on with the public nationwide. Bob remembered to include an invitation to K to contact him as a postscript.

People referred to K as His Eminence and speculated wildly about his real identity and purpose. Who was he? Who were the rebels? Was he connected with the Catholic Church, a query rising from the origins of the term Gray Eminence in 17th century Paris? Was he a Muslim agent? Was he even real? The entire world watched with bated breath.

Once the paper was out Bob got a call from Pete on his cell phone. He checked the number and answered it.

"Yeah?"

"How's it going?"

"Good. I never knew being on the lam could be so much fun."

"There's always a downside. Scanlon called. He wants to play a hand in the meeting if there is one. Should I give him your number?"

"Shit. If he gets my cell number I'll never be able to shake the guy. Give me his number and I'll call him on a land line."

Pete gave him the number and said, "He'll lean on you hard, Bob. He wants a piece of the action."

"So he can fuck it up with a daring midnight raid on the rebel headquarters accompanied by TV cameras for the evening news? No dice. If I can swing a deal I'll go solo as promised. We'll have dead politicians all over the place if Scanlon pulls some double cross that doesn't work."

"Like I said, he'll lean hard. Be ready."

"Forewarned is forearmed."

He hung up and punched Scanlon's number in on Colleen's phone and got an answer on the first ring.

"Scanlon."

"Ingersoll."

"Bob! Where the hell are you?"

"Forget that. And if you trace this call I'll never speak to your ass again."

"Listen, I read your column. It's perfect. I think K will bite."

"And if he does?"

"We track you on your cell phone. GPS. We also bug your car. You meet with K and we'll arrest the son-of-a-bitch five minutes after you get there."

"And what if K anticipates your plan and escapes? He'll never trust you again."

"It's fail-safe. What can go wrong? We'll follow you with radar, helicopters, GPS, an army of agents, enough firepower to capture Bin Laden…"

"No."

"No?"

"Yes, no."

"You can't say no to the F.B.I!"

"The hell I can't. I just did."

Scanlon shifted to a more plaintive mode. "Listen, Bob, you've got to leave this to the pros. This isn't some 7-Eleven stick up; we're talking national security, a threat to the safety of the entire nation, an armed rebellion, for Christ's sake. There's no way the government is going to let you play cops and robbers in a matter that involves national security."

"Look, I'm just a reporter, a great story comes along and I'm in the middle of it. What are the odds?

My job is to dig at the truth and tell my readers what I find. You're right, the nation is at stake, but it's the American people who are calling the shots. People out there really believe the country is severely fucked up and they're right. Maybe they're going about it in the wrong way but they want some changes that mean something, real changes in the way this country is run."

He stopped and took a deep breath. "You know, Scanlon, isn't there just a slight chance they may be right? Isn't it time we put a stop to all the crap and get America on track again?"

"You sound like you support the rebels. That would be treason, you know."

"Look, fuck it. I'm tired. I'm not making any bullshit deal with you guys. If K wants to meet I'll go alone or I won't go at all."

He hung up, dug a long roach from the ashtray, looked for and found a roach clip, applied flame to roach, and was instantly transported to more pleasant surroundings and cheerier prospects. A couple of more hits and he forgot all about rebellions and evil politicians and tight-assed feds and concentrated instead on Bach's Goldberg Variations pouring forth from a CD and drifted into something very close to bliss.

Scanlon was left to fume, politicians everywhere quaked in fear, the military/industrial complex conducted business as usual, the courts were silent, and the nation edgy. Their state of disorganization was revealed in a hastily called meeting at the Pentagon.

Every general and admiral still ambulatory in the

land or afloat on the sea descended on the building like Mayflies on a storefront window. Of course, uniforms featuring eight- or nine-pounds of gold braid made them look like a convention of doormen and much embarrassment resulted when visitors asked them to flag a cab or hold the door open.

Four-star general Walt Wisper summoned them to a huge auditorium where they were to address the current rebellion and plan a strategy. It was a top-secret meeting open only to top brass, but there was a brief disturbance half-way through when it was learned that half-a-dozen doormen had wandered in when they saw all the other doormen filing in and had heard all the classified stuff said there. In the end the interlopers were whisked away to some mysterious place and never seen again.

Once assembled and the doors secured, Gen. Wisper took the podium and recapped the events in a booming voice. When finished he called for suggestions from the audience and hands shot up everywhere. Wisper pointed at Adm. Scuttle, a windy old fool with a nose incarnadined by booze.

The admiral rose unsteadily and said, "We need more ships is what we need. More submarines, too. And three more aircraft carriers. These rebels might strike anywhere…"

Some beneficent soul cut off his mike and Wisper pointed at Gen. Custard, an obese man with two spare chins and so much braid even his colleagues thought he was a doorman. He rose and those nearby thought they heard his chair sigh.

"Mr. Chairman, I propose we initiate the draft at

once. Now, I know some people will object to that but here's my plan. If we draft every military-aged man in the country we'll have all the rebels in the army where we can watch 'em so they won't have a chance to do mischief."

A murmur swept the crowd and heads nodded approval even though the plan was obviously absurd. The brass will always like any plan that increases the size of our armed forces and their own importance. The fact that said plan is unworkable or will totally waste billions is never a factor. The Chair noted the suggestion and it was duly recorded in the minutes but never considered as a possibility because the president had sworn that he would never call for a draft and we all know he's a man of his word.

Other ideas were floated. Every idea promulgated by an admiral involved water in some form as the best means of combating insurrectionists, generals favored doubling the officer ranks and raising pay to attract the best people, and the air force wanted to bomb Kansas and South Dakota to "…teach the rebels a lesson…" though how the rebels would benefit from this wasn't made clear.

After considerable parleying discussion slowed as they began to run out of ideas. Finally, one more astute than the others took them on another track.

Gen. Hans Krager, a stern man who favored shiny boots and swagger stick à la Patton, rose and said, "Nobody is talking about the real problem here. For one thing we don't know who the enemy is so we can't stop him with armies and tanks. Where would we attack? And whom? But the main point is the so-called enemies are Americans. Do we fight the Civil War again? Would we kill fellow Americans for any reason?

"Maybe there's another way around this. We could try negotiations. Listen to their grievances." He trailed off and stopped talking and an uncomfortable silence crept through the large room and then slipped out again when the audience stirred.

"He's right," someone sang out. "It's not the same thing as killing Arabs."

"Yeah, but what if the president orders us to attack suspected rebels? Isn't that our duty?"

"The president *is* the commander-in-chief, isn't he?"

"But what if the president's a goddamn idiot?"

"Sir, we attack anyway!"

"Then *we're* goddamn idiots!"

Wisper held his hand up and called loudly for their attention. "Gentlemen, we're getting into very deep water here," he said ominously. "May I remind you that we don't have to attack anybody; all we have to do is make sure nobody can attack us. Now, to do that we will need more aircraft carriers, more planes and tanks and personnel and at least a trillion dollar budget and more perks for flag officers…" and so on with a veritable cornucopia of good stuff for advancing careers.

This speech won the audience over and all were convinced they'd come up with a solid plan to thwart the rebels and save America. They appointed a committee to work out the details of exactly how they'd protect the nation in a plan that would eventually be 800 pages long and make no sense whatever. All players were satisfied they'd done yeoman's work and everybody split for his villa, mansion, penthouse, or yacht while the committee members sat down to eviscerate the nation's inner workings and further despoil the people.

Oh, one of the real doormen climbed into a stretch limo with half-a-dozen admirals and rode off with them. He wasn't discovered for six months and by then the brass was embarrassed lest people find out they were such bozos they couldn't tell a doorman from an admiral and they let him keep the job. The guy was later promoted and retired on a handsome pension on the condition that he keep his trap shut and he did.

CHAPTER TEN

Three days passed without further word from K but the president broke his silence that evening with a broadside fired at the would-be rebels. He gave a speech in prime time that drew the largest audience ever for any event in the entire world. Of course, he had no real understanding of what was going down but that didn't deter him. He wore his usual smirk, assumed a cocky attitude, and dismissed the revolutionaries as a mere lunatic fringe group that would quickly be broken up by the military. He challenged them to bring it on, to face the wrath of an angry government, and swore that anyone taking part in an armed rebellion against the United States would be arrested, charged with treason, and hanged.

Americans watched in astonishment, eyes wide and mouths agape in wonder. A revolution! The people at war with the government! Threats of reprisal, a call to arms, a cloud descending on the nation and shutting out reason and common sense in favor of violence and insanity. The topic drove all other subject matter off TV and the talk shows nationwide, the press printed no other news, people talked about nothing else; many were frightened, many angry, no one indifferent.

Even so, many Americans felt a sense of glee at the thought of the arrogant bastards having the tables turned on them for a change. Let the fuckers cover and run, see how it feels to be on the receiving end of abuse and oppression. Strip them of their health insurance, take away their egregious pensions, confiscate their illegal gains, which is to say all of their money, and make them live on their Social Security. What could be fairer than turnabout?

MoveOn signed up a million new members, money poured in to support the rebel cause, public approval shot up day by day. There was a run on tar producers, feather firms, and rail manufacturers across the land, and pots of burning tar simmered and bubbled while posses of Minutemen cruised the neighborhoods looking for stray politicos to tar and feather.

Gun stores sold out their entire stock in a week as people armed themselves either to help kill crooked politicians or defend themselves against anticipated attacks by rebels or U.S. Marines. Once the supply of guns ran out the unarmed freaked and ran around pleading for guns from friends they knew belonged to the NRA, friends they'd formerly derided as gun nuts and Second Amendment fanatics, but to no avail. They didn't get so much as a spent cartridge and had to rely on their wits to defend themselves, which means that many of them would only be half-safe.

The rest of the world all shared one view: they loved it. Al Jazeera ran a mini-series on the subject and Muslims everywhere were overjoyed. They were so excited they even voted to cancel their annual pilgrimage to Mecca and stopped shooting each other for almost a week.

Mexicans interpreted the rebellion as weakness on the government's part and millions more were encouraged to move in with all their relatives and further compound our problems. The Mexican government helped by starting a super highway that would run straight through the center of Mexico and directly to New York City. Our government's reaction was to offer a no-bid contract to Halliburton for two trillion dollars to build the highway—with illegal immigrant workers, of course.

Canada sent 500 soldiers to guard 3,000 miles of border against incursions by rabid dissenters that might leak over into their country and fuck them up, too. Haiti cut off all aid to America, Cuba prepared to invade Miami but changed plans when they found out they already owned it, and the Virgin Islands refused to allow American tourists who weren't Virgins.

The president's defiance would have seemed courageous except that the man had clearly shown courage wasn't an important part of his make up. He would never live down his desertion from the Texas Air National Guard during a time of war, a cowardly act that would shame any man of conscience. Everyone waited for K to drop the other shoe and they hadn't long to wait.

On the fourth day Rep. Will Wurst, Chairman of the Appropriations Committee and former CEO of a major credit card company, awoke in his sunlit bedroom and stretched mightily. He had a leisurely breakfast, showered, donned a $4,000 cashmere suit, and left on his way to the airport where a private corporate jet waited to take him to Las Vegas for a meeting with his associates. He was carrying a briefcase stuffed full of bundled $100 bills that had somehow gotten dirty and needed a good scrubbing.

The lawmaker's limo pulled up at his home. He

walked from the front door toward the car when a lone figure suddenly appeared moving very quickly. Wurst saw the man approach and his first thought was to chide him for trespassing when the bullet crashed into his forehead and killed him. He had no second thought.

The shooter snatched up the briefcase, strode to the driver's side, stopped and looked at him and said, "Wait five minutes." He turned and quickly disappeared into a grove of trees.

The shaken driver waited the full five minutes and felt no guilt because he could see the inert form of the very dead politician on his side, head thrown back and the by now traditional forehead hole in full view. Clearly, there was no need to hurry.

The news swept the world with every TV set tuned into what was fast becoming the first worldwide soap ever with a story that involved intrigue, politics, guns and violence, considerable humor, and reality that would shame the most acclaimed reality TV show ever seen. Real people doing real things in front of billions of viewers every day with very real potential outcomes that could actually change the course of everybody's history. It was, in fact, the story, of the century.

Viewers took sides, had favorite characters and knew every player. Bloggers wrote daily plot summaries complete with criminal records, number of divorces, military records, if any, major contributors, voting records, and more. Many legislators were so disgraced by their exposure that they resigned their positions and left town, often transported on a rail by helpful neighbors.

Everybody rooted for the rebels, even the Christians. While they usually vote for Christ, this time they voted against the Devil in the White House and his minions in Congress because they had to get evil out before they could replace it with good. There was some concern among ecclesiastics that Satan might refuse to accept the crooked bastards in hell, but we'll leave that for the Jesuits to resolve because they're skilled in specious thinking.

On the plus side interest in politics and government soared worldwide as teenagers hung copies of Delacroix's Liberty Storming the Barricades on bedroom walls and wore T-shirts from New Hampshire. Even university students rediscovered politics. It was suddenly chic to be a political science major and walk around with a rolled-up newspaper in hand like Mort Sahl in olden times.

In fact, the atmosphere was very like that of the '60s and '70s. No radical changes in clothing, as it would be hard for clothing to be much more radical than it has been of late, but the same passion and sense of involvement and desire for meaningful change that motivated hippies then and freethinking, intelligent people always.

Despite Pope's observation on hope, people still like to think things really can be better and that they can even play a part in the process. The rioters of the '60s and '70s felt that and in the end they did affect the course of history with their protests, pot-shrouded smoke-ins, garish costumes, and gaudily painted school buses pointing the way to a better world.

The upshot of all this was that the president threw

down the gauntlet and K picked it up and slapped him with it. It was plain that the rebellion would continue until the government agreed to address the rebel demands and it was equally clear that the president would stand firm just as he had with the war in Iraq because he had God on his side while the heathen Muslims only had Mohammad, a maker of tents and sixth-century troublemaker.

And so things escalated.

CHAPTER ELEVEN

With a stage set as this one was it wasn't surprising that would-be actors started appearing everywhere to pontificate on the situation and claim their share of the limelight. Normally, the pols would do all the talking but most of them were afraid to show themselves for fear of being shot. As a result, the talkers were academics, media people, celebrities, business types, et al., and the subject was always the same: what do we do about the rebellion?

While Bob had valiantly resisted being swept up in the furor, he found himself more and more the center of attention as the days passed. Since nobody had more involvement than he, people went to him even though he never had any new information for them. It got to where he avoided the media more because he felt like an idiot for always reciting the same handful of facts over again than just because the whole thing irritated him.

For example, he was hailed before a Senate sub-committee investigating the rebellion and recent events and he felt like an attorney general answering every question with I don't know or I can't recall.

"...seen K?"

"No."

"Has he ever communicated with you in any way other than the U.S. mail?"

"No."

"Do you know where K is?"

"No."

"Have you ever met anyone in his organization?"

"I didn't know there was an organization."

"It doesn't seem to you that there must be an organization of some sort?"

"I don't know."

"Have you ever met a rebel?"

"Many times but not in connection with K."

"Do you think K will meet with you?"

"I don't know."

"What is your guess?"

"I think not. He seems to have his own agenda."

"In your view, what action do you think the government should take in dealing with this disturbance?"

"Probably negotiate. You'll gain more by talking than you will by fighting a civil war. Besides, people always end up negotiating these things. Why not just go right to the talking part and skip the war part? At least there's a chance you might save lives with words rather than bullets."

"What is your personal view on the rebellion? Do you support the rebels?"

"I support the side that's best for the American people."

"Sir! Do you realize that's tantamount to treason?"

"No, it isn't. It's just my opinion."

"You haven't been too forthcoming, Mr. Ingersoll. Are you holding anything back? Have you told us everything you know about this matter?"

"I have."

The committee members huddled for a minute or

two and took turns raising their heads and peering intently at Bob. At last they declared the hearing over and everyone left the room feeling it had all been a waste of time. This didn't upset the senators all that much, as wasting time was one of the things they did well, but it did upset Bob and put him back in hiding for the next couple of days.

Fortunately, nobody had wised up to Colleen's place and having her around made his self-imposed exile much less imposing. He did, however, miss going out on the town or even just for dinner, but it was by no means durance vile. In fact, he began to enjoy lazing about all day watching TV or reading, coffee at hand accompanied by smoke and fanciful thoughts.

On the second day after the hearing Bob got a call from editor Pete.

"Yes?"

"Mail came. There's another letter from your pen pal."

"No shit!"

"Want me to open it?"

"Uh, no. It may have stuff he doesn't want to share yet. I'll be right there."

He flipped the phone shut, took another sip from the day's seventh cup of coffee, grabbed a handful of grapes and his jacket and was en route to the paper in less than a minute.

This time he drove past the posted sentinels and straight into the company lot and into a spot marked with his name. By the time the startled lookouts recognized him he was entering the building and beyond their grasp. He raced non-stop to Pete's office and his latest rendezvous with destiny.

Pete was alone with a single envelope resting on the desk in front of him. It was identical to the earlier envelopes with the same return address but this time posted from Baltimore.

Bob closed the door and approached it warily, as though half expecting it to explode. He looked at Pete who looked back and slid the envelope toward him. Bob picked it up and turned it in his hands as if looking for clues then dropped into a chair and tore open one end of the envelope. He shook out the usual single sheet of stationery and peered inside to make sure it was empty, laid the envelope down, and unfolded the letter.

It was terse, same font, signature. Bob read it at a glance and then reread it to be sure he hadn't missed anything the first time. It read: Call me at 888-555-6164. Please do not involve the authorities yet. K

Bob handed the letter to Pete. He read it and looked up. "He wants to meet!"

Bob nodded. "Looks like it."

"Well?"

"I'm good. That's what we hoped for, isn't it?"

"What about Scanlon?"

"He says no cops yet."

"What's with the yet part?"

"I don't know. He must have some sort of timeline in mind." Bob took the letter from Pete and studied it. "A thought. Is it a crime if I don't give the letter to the feds? It's my mail addressed to me. Do I have to give it to him before I meet K?"

"Good question. Let's run it by legal." He picked

up the phone and said, "Helen, get me Ed Shade. Tell him its urgent. Yeah." He hung up and Bob tossed the letter back to him.

"File this. Scanlon will want it."

"He isn't the only one. The whole world is waiting for this letter. They want the next installment."

"Better safe than sorry."

"I don't blame you. Nobody's safe now with all this terrorism crap going on. One false move and you could find your ass on a midnight flight to Egypt."

The phone rang and Pete answered it. "Yes?"

"Ed, Pete. What's up?"

"Got a question for you. Top secret stuff. Got a spare minute?"

"Sure. I got a quick meeting here... I'll be there in an hour."

"Good." He hung up. "Ed will be here at two."

"I'm hungry. Let's do lunch."

So they repaired to a nearby diner where Pete had a fat corned beef sandwich with a medium-sized pickle that resembled a dildo while Bob made do with a veggie cheeseburger on a hemp bun and a mug of steaming java. They studiously avoided talk about K both to avoid being overheard and because they needed a respite from rebels and gray eminences and federal cops. After a leisurely hour they started back to the paper and ran into attorney Shade on his way in.

"Top secret stuff, eh?" Shade said. "Sounds intriguing."

"We're trying to keep Bob out of jail."

"Hmm. That's even more intriguing. What's he done?"

Pete withheld further information until they were in his office. He took the letter from his desk drawer and held it out to the attorney. "Attorney-client privilege applies, right?"

"Right." He took the letter, read it, and looked up. "From K? Jesus Christ, you weren't kidding! Even the air around this envelope is top secret!" He tossed the letter on the desk and Pete picked it up

Bob said, "You mean it's classified?"

"The only thing with a higher classification in Washington is the president's Vietnam War service record."

Pete dropped the letter as if it had suddenly burst into flames. "Holy shit!"

"Talk about Top Secret!" Bob said. "But the question is, do I have to turn it over to the feds? Or can I meet with K and give 'em the letter afterwards?"

"Hmm. Well, this letter isn't classified yet because they don't know it exists. On the other hand, everything about the investigation is classified..." He trailed off and thought for a moment. "First, if they want to the feds could claim you aided and abetted the enemy and pack you off to Cuba under the Patriot Act. They could keep you there forever as a enemy combatant but they won't do that because they need you."

"That's scary as hell," Pete said. "All we need now is our very own Gulag and a kangaroo court judicial system."

"We already have that in the federal rendition program," Shade said. "The feds outsource torture to Egypt and other enlightened societies so they can say we don't torture people. It's illegal, unconstitutional, and counterproductive but they do it, anyway. Still, I think you've got 'em by the balls, Bob. You're the only one K talks to so you're holding trump cards. I say take the meeting and turn the letter over as soon as you get back. That leaves the feds stuck with a fait accompli."

"That's it, then," Bob said. He picked up the phone. "I'll set it up before he changes his mind."

He punched in the numbers and waited through four rings before a voice said, "Yes?"

"Bob Ingersoll."

Silence, then, "Noon tomorrow. The Lincoln Memorial. Please come alone. No media, no police."

The line went dead and Bob lowered the phone. "We meet tomorrow."

"Maybe you should tell the feds," Shade said. "If K is the ringleader they may be able to round up the rest of 'em and nip this whole revolution thing in the bud."

Bob shook his head. "No cops. I gave my word."

"It's risky."

"No, it isn't. He can't shoot me in front of the Lincoln Memorial."

"Don't agree with him on anything," Shade advised. "You don't want to be complicit. Whatever he says or offers just agree to act as a go-between to take the information to Scanlon. No deals, no promises. Whatever you say or do in the meeting will come out later when this thing gets thrashed out in court."

"Got it. I'll play my cards close to my vest."

Shade rose to leave. "Let me know how it goes tomorrow. And give me a call if you need some legal muscle."

Bob looked at Pete. "You pay for my lawyer, right?"

Pete smiled the smile of a man who sees a rosy-fingered dawn in his immediate future. "Don't worry, you're covered."

Shade left and so did Bob. He'd had enough intrigue for the day and longed for the safety of Colleen's comforting arms and four walls sans media.

Bob wrote the next day's column but didn't mention the latest development for obvious reasons. He did hint that something new might be in the offing but it was subtle and vague enough not to draw suspicion, at least not with most people.

Scanlon, however, was not most people. It was his nature to be suspicious even when there was no need for it. He reread the piece three times and each time had the same sense that it was saying more than was in the actual words. After the third reading he decided to pay a visit to the paper to quiz Bob again and probe around for any inconsistencies. He left for the paper just before lunch but missed Bob because he was on his way to the Lincoln Memorial and a long awaited meeting with the infamous K.

Scanlon approached the editor's office and was ushered into the inner sanctum where Pete toiled on future editorials. He looked up as Scanlon entered.

"What brings you here unannounced?"

"Business. Is Bob in?"

"No. You needed to see him?"

"It's nothing, just routine. Do you know where I can find him?"

"A question. I hear it's a felony to lie to an F.B.I. agent. Is that true?"

"That's a fact. You can serve time for it."

"Okay, then our conversation is over."

"So you do know where he is?"

Pete grinned. "No comment."

"Listen, you can also serve time for refusing to answer an agent's questions."

"That's bullshit and you know it."

Scanlon shrugged. "Yeah, I know but it was worth a try."

"You got a new wrinkle on the case?"

"No. I thought I might get one from Bob. I don't suppose he's come up with anything new, has he?"

"No comment."

"You're a slippery bastard, Schevo," Scanlon said, admiration in his voice. "I like that in a man. Shows he's on top of his game."

"Or it shows you're hanging out with the wrong crowd. You only have to be slippery when dealing with duplicitous people."

"Maybe that's where I get it," Scanlon sighed. "Everybody I deal with in this job is duplicitous." He turned to go and then stopped. "You will have him call me when he gets back?"

Pete raised his eyebrows and held up his hands but said nothing. Scanlon grunted and left.

Meanwhile, Bob reached the Memorial and loitered around out front for a few minutes without result. He wore a baseball cap with the bill riding low on his face and kept his head down to lessen the chance that a fan would recognize him and screw-up the meeting with autograph requests, etc., even though nobody ever asked him for an autograph before. Still, it could happen and he garnered some satisfaction from that. After a few minutes he sat on a nearby bench and tried to look touristy.

Some twenty minutes later he was half drowsing when he suddenly realized someone was sitting on the bench next to him. Quickly alert, he turned and gazed into the face of K for the first time. It was a memorable moment, so much so that Bob was tempted to look around for Iwo Jima's Joe Rosenthal with camera poised amid martial music.

The Gray Eminence was anything but gray. One could tell he was a tall man even while sitting with jutting knees, long arms, and angular face. He wore a good suit, close-cropped full white beard, and what looked like a saber scar on his left cheek that actually resulted from an unfortunate experience with a barbwire fence as a boy. The short buzz haircut, deep blue eyes, and chiseled features added to his overall resemblance to a German U-boat commander from central casting. The fact that he was also of German extraction may have played a role here.

He offered his hand. "Kessler. Fritz Kessler."

Bob turned to face him and took his hand. "A.k.a. K?"

Kessler smiled a warm smile. "The very same." He looked around. "No police hiding in the bushes?"

"You said to come alone."

"Yes, I did." He looked steadily at Bob. "Why you? I read your column and I know your views, your position on political matters, your humanitarian interests…"

"Humanitarian interests?"

"They show in your writing. Beyond that, I know you read The Nation and Progressive, always vote Democratic, and support liberal causes. You're on the side of the workingman and favor strong unions and national health care. In other words, you're one of us."

"Us? Who are us?"

"Average Americans. The people, the man on the street. The middle-class American who gets poorer as the rich get richer. The country has become the private property of special interest groups, lobbyists, and crooked politicians. The people are the ones angry enough to kill them."

"So you're for real. You really are an insurrectionist!"

"No. I'm an attorney. I practiced law in Los Angeles, civil law. I made enough to give up my practice and work on other matters that I enjoy more."

"Like leading a full-scale rebellion against the government?"

"I'm not leading anything. I merely offer pro bono services to Americans trying to regain their country, their rights, and liberties. That's the extent of my involvement."

"I'm not sure the feds will buy that, Mr. Kessler."

"Please call me Fritz."

"Is it safe to be on a first-name basis with a revolutionary?"

"Would you have befriended George Washington?"

"Surely, you're not…"

"Of course not. We do share the same goals, though.

Revolutionary means different things to different people. The usual rule is that successful rebels are admired while unsuccessful rebels are hanged."

"Are you worried that you might be hanged?"

Kessler fixed him with a steely stare and said, "Bob, if we don't do something to reform this government we'll all be hanged, metaphorically if not literally. They'll strip the people of their independence, self-esteem, and pride. These are the new Intolerable Acts; we mustn't tolerate them. If they can't be stopped peacefully, they must be stopped another way."

"Tell me, why Republicans? So far they're the only ones being killed. Do the rebels hate them more than the Dems?"

Kessler sighed and looked left and right to check for feds lurking in nearby bushes. "Class warfare. Societies are always divided by wealth and poverty so we always have at least two parties. The GOP helps the rich get richer and fights to keep the lower classes poor and out of sight.

"Think the Iraq War, the Bankruptcy Bill to help credit card companies, the phony prescription drug program with doughnut holes, resistance to national health care, free trade agreements that benefit the rich and hurt working Americans, job outsourcing, election fraud, no-bid contracts to Halliburton, anti-labor laws, privatizing Social Security, eliminating Medicare…"

"And the Dems?"

"They align themselves with the middle class, with working people and the poor. Now think 40-hour week, overtime pay, paid vacations, health coverage, unemployment benefits, Social Security, Medicare, labor unions, prevailing wage laws, Fair Employment Practices Act, the Disabilities Act, the Civil Rights Act, and many more. All of these programs came about because of the Democratic Party."

"It's too bad those guys in Kansas don't know all this."

"They're fools. Any middle-class person who votes Republican is a fool. The same holds for minorities, as the GOP traditionally hates people of color. Few things are more pathetic than the sight of an African-American at a Republican rally. Besides, studies show Republicans are less attractive than Democrats, probably due to the predatory look one often sees in their eyes. If you see a pretty girl, the odds are she's a Democrat.

"But it's more than that. Republicans tend to be selfish, even greedy—and outright mean. People have no health insurance and they don't care. The poor live in squalor and billionaire Steve Forbes whines because he's over taxed."

"You're right. Every time I see that asshole on TV he's bitching about high taxes and demanding they pass a flat-rate tax so he can get even richer."

Kessler shrugged. "Exactly. Republicans lack humanitarian instincts, empathy, and compassion. Reagan put mental patients on the street because it was cheaper than housing them. The president deliberately started a war and then cut benefits for the troops fighting it to save money for his ballooning budget. He even vetoed health insurance for poor children. Intolerable."

"All this sounds good but do you have to assassinate

half of Congress to change things?"

Kessler didn't answer. Instead, he looked around warily and said, "I want you to call a press conference for me next week. On Saturday. Choose a venue that's suitable, one large enough to accommodate a crowd. I imagine a great many people will want to attend. Send the top political leaders special invitations and announce a temporary truce so that they can attend without fear of being shot. You have my number. Let me know where and when."

He stood and so did Bob. "Jesus Christ, you've just asked me to arrange the biggest press conference in the history of the whole goddamn world!"

"Yes, isn't that remarkable?" He smiled and offered his hand. "Thanks for coming."

Bob grinned back. "Thank you for giving me the story of the century!"

Kessler turned and moved off, his tall form slightly bent as against the wind, and disappeared into a crowd of tourists sweeping past on their way to the next wonder on their itinerary.

Suddenly, Bob felt his knees buckle and he plopped back on the bench and stared after the departed rebel while his brain whirled and spat and finally shorted out and left him breathless and drained. He fumbled in his shirt pocket and brought forth a joint and began searching for a match when a hand came into view holding a lighter. He looked up and saw a smiling black man wearing a red and yellow worker's vest and holding shears in one hand.

"You are going to light that fatty, aren't you?" he said.

Bob smiled back and said, "Why, yes, as a matter of fact, I am. Would you care to join me?"

And so it happened that ace investigative reporter Bob Ingersoll shared a smoke with a smiling black man on a warm afternoon in front of the Lincoln Memorial and things continued apace.

CHAPTER TWELVE

After Kessler left Bob he took a cab to the law offices of Kelley and Keene, one of the most prominent law firms in the city. The firm was in a high-rise structure with offices that covered an entire upper floor. The place looked like it had been furnished as an art museum with paintings on the walls that would make curators salivate. Persian carpets were in evidence along with Tiffany lamps and tables by Maloof and Nakashima, and even a suit of medieval armor. If the intent was to impress visitors it was a smashing success.

Kessler approached the receptionist, clearly a runway model taking a respite from the arduous work of being admired by others, and asked to meet with Mr. Kelley himself. The receptionist was momentarily rattled as no one had ever asked that before.

"Mr. Kelley?"

"Yes."

"Have you an appointment?"

"No."

"I'm sorry, sir, but Mr. Kelley never sees anyone without an appointment."

"He'll see me. Tell him I've come to give him ten million dollars."

"Ten...? Uh, just a moment, sir." She punched in a number on the phone and said, "Martha, I have a Mr. Kessler for Mr. Kelley. No. But he says he wants to give Mr. Kelley ten million dollars. Yes." She hung up.

"One moment, sir." A moment later the phone buzzed and she answered it. "Yes? Thank you. You may go in, sir."

Kessler entered the door marked Private and found himself in an interior office with a receptionist of its own apparently named Martha. She smiled a smile that would have gladdened a heart of stone and rose to usher him into the great man's presence personally.

E. C. Kelley's office had a sweeping view of all creation and was large enough to house a good part of it. He crouched behind a huge desk with his arms on its surface and eyed his visitor warily.

Kessler strode straight to the desk and reached across it. "Kessler, sir, Fritz Kessler."

Kelley took his hand and shook it without taking his eyes from Kessler's face, but he smiled broadly at the same time. "A pleasure, sir. I understand you want to give me ten million dollars, Mr. Kessler?"

"That's true, but only indirectly. What I can give you is access to such a sum and much more." He paused for dramatic effect and then said, "I am K."

For a split second Kelley missed the connection but then his eyes widened and he sat bolt upright in his chair with body language indicating he was totally flummoxed by the news. "K?" he managed to say.

"Yes, K."

"Great God!"

"No, just Fritz Kessler, attorney-at-law representing the American people and the cause of liberty and freedom."

"But what…uh, what…?"

Kessler sat down, crossed his legs, and made himself

at home. "It's simple. I need legal representation, or I will in a few days, anyway. I've called a press conference for Saturday and I'm not sure how that's going to come out. I need someone to keep them from shipping me to Cairo on their rendition program and that will require the most powerful legal team I can muster."

"Yes, yes, of course. You came to the right place, sir. But you mentioned ten million dollars..."

"I'm not a poor man, Mr. Kelley. I handled some large class action suits and made a lot of money, more money than I need. But business is business, after all, so I offer you a deal. Your firm keeps me from being swept under the rug and in return my case makes yours the best-known law firm in the world. We could end up in court and four or five billion people will see Kelley and Keene in action. There will doubtless be lawsuits galore and your firm will handle them. You'll want to expand your international branches because business will go through the roof as soon as this is announced."

"And you pay...?"

"I'll pay a fee of $1,000,000 to your firm and contribute another $3,000,000 to Wayne State University's scholarship fund. That's my alma mater, by the way. I get legal representation, your firm earns hundreds of millions, and some poor, deserving kids in Detroit get an education. Everybody wins."

"Mr. Kessler, you have your legal team. Give me a dollar for consideration and you are an official client. I'll handle your case personally, sir."

And so Kessler anticipated trouble and took steps

to head it off at the well-known pass. As it turned out this was a clever move on his part.

The next day's headline shouted in bold type, GRAY EMINENCE UNMASKED! and readers were sent to Bob's account of his meeting with the mysterious K and his call for a press conference. Major news stories were relegated to the back pages, pundits wrote of nothing else, the evening news was expanded to an hour almost by public demand, and Bob feared for his life and fled to Colleen's as the only safe haven left to him.

These fears were not entirely unfounded. Some were pissed at Bob for not calling the cops and arresting Kessler when he had the chance and implied he might be one of the conspirators and should be dealt with. Some actual threats came in to the paper but most seemed written by morons and didn't pose real danger.

But even more frightening was the possibility that the crowds clamoring to get a look at him could crush him to death. On one occasion he had to run at full tilt to escape what seemed to him the Charge of the Light Brigade and he only got away by ducking into a department store and hiding in ladies' lingerie until the mob thinned out and he could leave via the loading dock.

For these reasons Bob laid low through most of the week before the press conference but others were more active. The state department was flooded with requests for emergency credentials and finally simply closed its doors and sent everybody home because all knew it was impossible to do its work.

Thousands of cops were flown in from both coasts to help with security, army units were dispatched to points surrounding the city and soldiers lined every street in full battle gear, storefront windows were boarded up, residents left town in droves to escape what many thought would be the start of the promised Rapture.

Every other person on the streets of D.C. during that week was a media type with mike and/or notebook ever at the ready. Reporters interviewed everybody they could get to stand still for two minutes, everyone had an opinion on the rebellion, many claimed to know rebels personally and offered to introduce reporters to them but few took them up as it was clear these folks were mostly idiots.

The venue chosen for the upcoming press conference was an outdoor stage in the National Mall where thousands could fan out over several acres and still see the stage via large TV screens strategically placed in the area. TV cameras would send the signal to every part of the Earth's surface, radio broadcasts would reach the spots TV missed, camel, donkey riders, and solitary hikers would carry the news to the six or seven spots not covered by any of the above.

Huge tents were thrown up near the stage where banks of hundreds of microphones were set up for foreign correspondents to broadcast the proceedings in dozens of languages. Interpreters mixed with technicians and reporters and hangers-on who called back and forth in languages that would have baffled the folks at Berlitz headquarters. Exotic costumes from countries not on any map appeared everywhere, parties broke out on street corners and in parking lots, and a bizarre kind of Mardi Gras grew until it engulfed the city and suburbs and the world marveled.

Rebellion business soared on other fronts. Hawkers sold T-shirts featuring cloaked and hooded gray figures with the words Gray Eminence on them while local businesses that weren't boarded up offered Gray Eminence specials on commodities from ice cream to cigars and beyond. Unnoticed others stroked their chins and plotted ways to capitalize on the phenomenon including toy companies, clothing lines, stockbrokers, filmmakers, et al.

The world's eyes were on the city for the entire week. Minute by minute reports were fired off into space at the speed of light and eagerly followed by everyone everywhere. People poured into the city and environs in an endless stream of planes, buses, cars, and filled all available space with their luggage. There wasn't a single room to rent in the metropolitan area at any price.

Tens of thousands bunked down in doorways, parks, their cars and RVs, on rooftops and in alleyways and created traffic jams where streets were literally parking lots with drivers out of their cars and lounging about reading newspapers and cooking hot dogs. The police would have sorted all this out but they couldn't get through the human thicket to reach the trouble spots.

By Saturday morning the restless throng edged closer to the National Mall and stood thousands deep in the park itself. Police were everywhere but largely unneeded as the huge crowds reminded many of the peaceable assembly of half-a-million dopers at Woodstock in '69. The party atmosphere was replaced with a somber mood more in keeping with the serious nature of the business at hand.

As the announced time drew near Bob, wearing a hat and dark glasses, came down from the stage and moved along the edge of the crowd nearest it. He scanned the throng and then quickly approached it, reached in and took Kessler's arm, and pulled him from the crowd as he waved his official pass at those closest to make way for him.

He led Kessler to the stairs and up onto the stage and gave him a gentle shove toward the center where a standing microphone awaited. No one reacted as no one knew Kessler and assumed he was just another official with an announcement. He advanced to the microphone, stood quietly for a moment, and then said in a clear, strong voice, "My name is Fritz Kessler. I am K!"

There was a moment of stunned silence, then an aural explosion as a million people roared their approval. The sound waves rocked the stage and broke windows in the park with their force while billions of others worldwide added to the din that might have been heard on the moon it if weren't so far away.

And then it was over. No sooner had Kessler made his announcement than agent Scanlon and a dozen of his men stormed the stage, tackled Kessler and threw him down, cuffed his hands behind his back, and rushed him off the stage. In minutes they had slipped out the back way and sped off with their precious cargo.

Bob was horrified as was everybody else and then instantly horror changed to anger and the whole country went crazy a once. Riots sprang up across the land, pissed-off mobs stormed City Halls and demanded Kessler's release, troops were called and most joined the protesters because the troops were also pissed at being denied their long awaited look at the mysterious K.

Viewers worldwide were almost as angry as Americans were. Crowds gathered and demanded that Kessler be allowed to speak and compared the F.B.I. to Nazis except in Germany where the comparison was the Russian KGB. There was also a vast number that thought the Keystone Kops made the truest match and they were probably right.

The disruptions lasted all day Sunday and only cooled off with the start of the workweek on Monday but this didn't signify peace. People were still pissed about it and a clamor rose up demanding that K be brought back and allowed to address them and explain his plan and the rebellion itself. Everyone agreed that Scanlon and the F.B.I. had overplayed their hand and screwed up royally, but K was at least temporarily under wraps and that's what mattered to the feds.

CHAPTER THIRTEEN

Held prisoner in the back seat of an unmarked car and pinioned between two burly agents like bulky bookends on both sides of a single book, Kessler seemed unruffled by his seizure and arrest. In fact, he had anticipated it as a predictable reaction by the feds. The last thing they wanted was to provide him with a forum on national TV to propound his heretical views and possibly further his cause in the process.

It was in preparation for this event that he had hired Kelley & Keene days earlier. Even as he was en route to imprisonment powerful friends were rushing to his defense with briefcases bulging with mandamuses, torts, subpoenas, habeas corpus writs, injunctions, and similar tools of the legal trade. While he was not out of danger by any means, at least he might avoid the enemy combatant charge that would speed him off to God knows where and what.

They moved through masses of people looking to do mischief but they ignored the car because its windows were tinted and it was unmarked. Had they known Kessler was inside they'd have sprung him and done considerable damage to the car and the feds who'd kidnapped the planned entertainment and spoiled their day.

Thirty minutes later Kessler was safely ensconced in an interrogation room deep in the interior of F.B.I. headquarters and gazing into a large wall mirror that he assumed was two-way glass with slack-jawed agents measuring the cut of his jib on the other side. He looked calmly at the mirror and then turned his attention to the rest of the room for any signs of racks, thumb screws, tongs, garrotes, whipping posts, iron maidens, etc. and was relieved to find none. Of course, such items could well be in a basement dungeon where some masked galoot in leather would apply some or all of the above to induce his talking but at least they weren't starting out there.

He sat alone in a straight-backed wooden chair with his hands still handcuffed behind his back. After ten minutes the door opened and Scanlon entered with two other agents named Cal and Sharon. Sharon sat at a table with recording equipment on it and Cal took up his post near the door as if to prevent Kessler from escaping. Scanlon went behind him and released the handcuffs and Kessler massaged his wrists to restart circulation.

Scanlon sat down opposite him and said, "Sorry about the rough treatment back there. SOP, you know. Have to play it by the book."

"By whose book?"

"Our book, the Bureau's book. The rule book."

"There may be other editions, other versions and rules."

Scanlon leaned back and took a closer look at Fritz Kessler, a.k.a. K. "Are you the leader of an armed insurrection against the government of the United States of America?"

"I'll be glad to discuss anything you like that doesn't pertain to my case, but not a word on that subject without my attorneys present."

"You're taking the Fifth Amendment?"

"No, I'm only asking for my right to an attorney under the Sixth Amendment."

"You can't have an attorney. You're being charged as a terrorist under the Patriot Act and you are not entitled to legal representation."

"Really?"

"Is that all you have to say?"

"Yes."

Scanlon hesitated and looked at Cal but received no help from that quarter. He turned back to Kessler. "You know, you really are in deep shit here, Mr. Kessler."

"Of course I know it. That's why I want my attorneys."

"They could hold you indefinitely without charges."

"I suppose they could."

"If you cooperate with us the government would give you a break on your sentence."

Kessler was normally a patient man but he'd never suffered fools gladly even though it often redounded to his harm. He leveled his gaze on Scanlon and said, "The charges against me include murdering congressmen and leading an armed revolt against the government and you offer me a reduced sentence? Would the hangman lower the drop from twelve to eleven feet? Would the firing squad use smaller caliber bullets? You are a fool, sir, and we're done here."

Scanlon's face reddened and he clenched his fists. "Like hell we are!" he snarled. "Get him out of here!"

Cal sprang forward, reapplied the handcuffs, and

trundled his prisoner away. He looked at Scanlon as he passed him; neither said anything and nothing needed to be said.

Of course, Bob knew none of this as Kessler was being held incommunicado and Scanlon refused to answer his persistent phone calls. Then the Kelley and Keene team popped up and he learned they were representing Kessler. Armed with a place to go, he called the firm and was put through to Kelley.

"Mr. Ingersoll!" Kelley said. "I thought you might call."

"I just found out he hired you guys. What's the story? What have they done with him?"

"The F.B.I. still has him but we don't know exactly where. Probably still in the Hoover building where they'll interrogate him."

"Have you seen him?"

"Not yet, but we will tomorrow. They're holding a hearing and we're serving a habeas corpus writ and asking that bail be set."

"Is bail a given?"

"No, not in a case like this. But it's going to be okay. There's no evidence of any wrongdoing on Kessler's part, no witnesses or smoking guns. The feds are desperate, they need answers or somebody to arrest and he's the best possible lead they have now."

"The bastards will trick him or beat a confession out of him…!"

"Mr. Kessler is an attorney so it's unlikely they'll trick him with a good cop bad cop routine, and it's even less likely they'll beat a confession from him. I got the impression that he is a strong man who knows exactly what he's doing and won't be easily deterred."

Bob heaved an audible sigh and said, "I hope so. I like the guy. I don't hold with assassinations as a rule, but maybe he's right and it's time somebody did something."

"We like to believe in our clients—when we can, and I believe in Mr. Kessler. The rightness of his cause may be debated but he's sincere and honest, I'm convinced of that."

"Can I attend the hearing?"

"No. It will be closed. They claim national security. But I'll call you when it's over and fill you in on the details."

"Off the record. Does it look good?"

"I'd say so. Mr. Kessler is his own best defense; he'll be a match for them. I might add that I think he's innocent."

"Good luck tomorrow, counselor."

They hung up simultaneously with neither saying goodbye the way it's often done in the movies but seldom in real life, as it borders on rudeness. Bob was encouraged to know Kessler had good lawyers but still worried because he knew the government wouldn't play fair. With the denial of habeas corpus, no lawyer, no right to call witnesses or cross-examine accusers, secret trials by military tribunals in off-shore venues, no right of appeal one can simply disappear so completely you'd think David Blaine was doing another one of his sidewalk tricks.

It was reminiscent of Nazis and Gulags, of Star Chambers and Inquisitions and Red Scares. To be charged as a terrorist is to be convicted in the America of the early 21ˢᵗ century. What would our forefathers think?

Bob put all this in his column, which was now syndicated worldwide and translated into dozens of languages, and took up the fight for Kessler's right to be heard but still didn't endorse the rebellion itself because he really couldn't get behind the killings. After all, it's one thing to support the notion that a revolt against bad government isn't always a bad idea, but the insurgents have to prove their cause is just lest we end up encouraging loonies and half-wits.

Attorney Kelley called Bob as promised after the hearing the next day with a discouraging report. The presiding judge heard the evidence against the defendant, decided there was none, and promptly ordered him held over for trial without bail. He denied all rights and even waved a copy of the Patriot Act to reinforce his decision.

"Jesus Christ, does he go straight to Gitmo?" Bob said.

"Probably not. There's too much interest in this case to just bury it. Half the world is watching to see what happens here. We're a democratic country but how will we react to the rebellion? People expect us to be fair and follow the letter of the law and not to abuse our own citizens so we'll look bad internationally if we don't do the right thing."

"And the right thing is?"

"File charges. Hold a jury trial and apply the Bill of Rights. Bring in evidence if there is any. Let the jury decide. Every citizen is entitled to no less, and especially so when there are charges like inciting a revolution against the legal government, which is always a capital offense."

"Will they do that?"

"They will if enough pressure is brought to bear. It's all about politics with this Administration. If it's useful politically that's what they do."

"Assholes."

Kelley sighed. "Yes, they are."

"Is all this good for my column? Any caveats?"

"No. Write everything you know. Emphasize Kessler's loss of his civil rights. Insist he be allowed to speak in his own defense, everybody can relate to that."

"I'm not so sure," Bob said, his faith in the democratic process undergoing an all-out assault in recent weeks.

"We have work to do, Bob."

"In spite of all the hassle, it is one hell of a story, isn't it?"

"It's also the biggest legal case in the nation's history. We both have much to be grateful for."

"Okay, I've got a column to write."

"We'll talk later."

Things were more settled over the next several days while everybody waited to see which way the wind would blow. Kessler remained incommunicado in Hoover's Palace but he stuck to his guns and refused to talk to anyone. Scanlon grew more desperate with each passing hour and unrelenting pressure from above to pin the rap on Kessler and get the matter closed.

Bob was still hanging out at Colleen's place as the media had taken up permanent residence in the street outside his building even though he hadn't been seen there in many days. What's more, he was beginning to get accustomed to the presence of a pretty girl and the many comforts of domestic life he had heretofore held in low regard.

A more prescient man might have noticed subtle nuances that evaded Bob partly because of all the craziness going on and partly because said nuances were subtle, indeed. Meals usually eaten alone became social events where he had somebody to talk to. TV was now a duo activity where he watched girl programs he hardly knew were on the air before because Colleen's interests had to be accommodated. It was all new to him and not altogether unpleasant.

On the other hand, Colleen was more observant and ambivalent about it.

"You're going to have to start paying rent," she said one evening.

"Rent?"

"Yes. Now that you've moved in we should share expenses."

Bob was alarmed. "Have I moved in?"

"It looks like it."

"But it's just until things get back to normal."

"Do you really think things will ever be normal again for you?"

"Sure, once this rebellion thing is over…."

"Be for real, Bob. You're an international star. You'll have a Pulitzer when this is over and you'll write a best-selling book and win another one. There'll be movie rights and theatrical rights for your play and you'll be rich as Croesus and there will never be anything normal in your life again."

"Stop it, you're scaring me!"

"So you owe me some rent."

"I'm good for it. Put it on my tab."

"Since when do you have a tab?"

"Since you brought up this rent business."

"I'll let you work some of it off. You make dinner tonight."

"Deal. I'll make my special veggie burgers with a side order of sprouts and boiled parsnips."

Colleen sighed and started to get up. "No, you won't. I'll order Chinese."

And so Bob and Colleen sank slowly, imperceptibly into domesticity never before considered as a viable option by either of them. Or was one or both of them as unaware as they implied?

CHAPTER FOURTEEN

Now that the Gray Eminence was in jail our brave congresspersons shed their armored vests and helmets and assumed a more assertive mien. They began to appear in public again sans disguises and could be seen in local TV interviews where they made brave speeches about standing firm, the need for patriotic fervor, courage in our nation's hour of need, and so on. They even assembled a full House to vote themselves another pay raise, a sure sign that things were back to normal.

They didn't forget the rebellion, of course. They had the ringleader in the slammer but there were vicious thugs out there who had to be brought to justice. Toward this end a Senate sub-committee of equally vicious thugs met in secret to plan a course of action that would end the rebellion, kill all the rebels, and assure their own political futures.

The Hon. Larson E. Maloney, a thrice-indicted crook high on the rebels' hit list, headed the committee. His accomplices included Paul van Snoot, heir to a vast mining fortune and chairman of the Mining Affairs Committee; Horace Smithers, a timber baron and member of the Forestry Committee; and Peter T. Peters, an insurance tycoon and member of the Insurance Regulating Committee. All were devout Christians. Their leader, Ali Baba, was busy sacking a wing of the Pentagon and couldn't make the meeting.

Maloney set the tone of the meeting by violating

congressional rules against smoking on the premises when he lit a fine illegal Cuban cigar and befouled the air with smoke that cost about fifty-cents a puff. No one objected, as all of them were pros with lifetimes spent in smoke-filled rooms where they plotted the nation's ruin.

"Boys," Maloney said, "the good news is we raised our pay; the bad news is those fucking rebels are still out there. We've got to stop the fuckers before they rile everybody up and start a real goddamn revolution."

"We need to make an example of Kessler," Smithers said, his face the color of maple leaves in late fall.

"I say we hang his rebel ass!" Peters said, fists clenched as though he'd do it himself if he weren't so busy.

"Yeah, a public hanging," van Snoot said. "We could put it on TV. That'd show the bastards we mean business."

"I like the hanging idea," Maloney said, "but I'm not sure about the TV angle. When those Arab assholes run a tape of them sawing some poor sap's head off people get pissed. Maybe we should hang him in secret and just leak a few frames to the Internet."

"Okay, we're agreed," Peters said. "We hang the Gray Eminence. Now, what do we do about those rebels who killed our people?"

"Let's trick 'em!" Smithers said. "We offer them amnesty if they turn themselves in and then hang the lot of 'em!"

"Won't that piss people off?" van Snoot said. "I mean, if we go back on our word some might think we can't be trusted."

"But that's silly," Maloney said. "We're politicians; we go back on our word all the time. People even expect it."

"We could claim they tried to escape," Peters said.

"What?" van Snoot said. "And we used ropes to catch 'em?"

Maloney shook his head. "Naw, people would be suspicious."

Smithers had been lost in deep thought and suddenly saw a light. "How about this? We offer a huge reward—$25 million—if people turn a rebel in and when somebody does we hang the guy."

"Twenty-five mil?" Maloney said. "That would add up to a fortune if we had to pay that much for every rebel!"

"But we wouldn't," Smithers said. "Once we paid the first informer we could leak his name to the Internet and the other rebels would kill him and nobody else would turn any more in."

"But that way we'd only get one rebel," van Snoot protested.

"Yeah, but it would send a message to the rest of the fuckers. They'd be afraid somebody might blow the whistle on them."

"Maybe we could outsource the job," Peters said.

"You mean send the rebels to India?" Maloney said.

"How would you do that? You'd have to round 'em up first."

"Who? The Indians?"

"No, the rebels."

"Oh, yeah."

They lapsed into a silence broken only by Maloney's wheezing and Peters' soft drumming on the table. After a moment van Snoot said, "Maybe we could pay them off. Give each rebel a million dollars if he promises not to shoot any more of us."

"And when the rebels show up for their checks we could hang 'em!" Smithers said, elated that his idea was still alive.

"It didn't work in 1805."

"Or with Bin Laden. Nobody has collected his reward."

Drained by all this heavy thinking, their minds began to wander. Peters' brain was worn to a frazzle and he had trouble staying awake while van Snoot was anxious to leave as he had a meeting with the president to draw up a plan to raze a redwood forest and slash loggers' pay and benefits, a dream close to both their hearts. After a longish silence it was mutually agreed that they'd made real headway and they adjourned,

Of course, none of these ideas ever bore fruit. Bizarre hangings, double crosses, phony rewards, killing Medicare, outsourcing are long cherished Republican goals and popular with selfish, mean-spirited, ignorant and unscrupulous Conservatives forever on the lookout for a chance to abuse their fellow citizens in the name of profit and greed. Small wonder the abused are wont to murder their abusers.

The result was that nothing was done to apprehend the rebels because they simply couldn't find any. The shootings stopped since the aborted press conference, no more letters showed up, Kessler was in jail waiting to be hanged, and everything was kosher again.

But only momentarily. The day after the senatorial thugs sorted through their various plot options there were new casualties. Rep. Mike Spooner (R-CA) went to a large Indian casino to pick up his alleged winnings when he was found dead on the fifteenth hole of the championship golf course with an arrow in his black heart. The authorities didn't count it as a rebel act at first because the man wasn't shot in the head like the others, but the word spread quickly on the Internet that it was a rebel strike and the game was afoot again.

One could tell news of the latest attack had reached D.C. from the reappearance of helmets and armored vests on many of the pols. They would scuttle from pillar to pillar, sidle along the walls, look furtive and therefore all the more obvious as they sought to dodge their executioners.

However, some of the craftier ones elected deception and wit to befuddle would-be assassins with disguises. For example, old man Maloney wore a floppy hat, dark glasses, a cane, and a pretty nurse on his arm to pass as a very old and harmless codger. He loused up the image somewhat when he gave the nurse a friendly pat on her posterior as they entered the elevator, though.

Sen. Elwin Dancy (R-MI) wore a Lone Ranger-type mask but everybody knew who he was, anyway. Maybe it was because he often stood next to his pal Sen. Johnny Mohawk, a real life Cherokee Indian from Los Angeles. That and the genuine antique cigar store Indian he kept in his office.

One senator who shall be nameless —Hobson, (R-TN)—came to work wearing an ankle-length gown his mistress gave him and furthered the deception with high heels and a styled wig that made him look like Marie Antoinette.

This last is gauche, I know, but effective. Some of the peasants were seen to eye him suspiciously and some claim they were hiding pavers under their shirts. Fortunately, there were no cake jokes.

Anyway, everybody wore dark glasses, collars were turned up, moustaches shaved off or fake ones put on, hair dyed or restyled if a woman or gay, new body language adopted and all in an effort to thwart justice. Any killer would be hard pressed to locate a given target in a crowded hallway with any accuracy.

Of course, if one's main purpose is to shoot a politician, one could fire randomly into Capitol crowds and be sure of winging one or two of them on each outing. That would screw up the planned order of victims, though, with some of the better ones being shot before the worst of them and that wouldn't be fair since everybody knows rebels fighting oppressors are always fair-minded and honest men with the good of the people their only concern.

Yes, it's true that some scheming thug will emerge soon after a successful coup, murder half the population and enslave the rest, and a year or two later new rebels will rendezvous in cellars to throw the new guys out and the dance goes on. The proper role for a wise man is that of observer, a witness; these dramas always play out the same way.

The president reacted to the latest assassination by redoubling his guard and closing the drapes in the Oval Office lest some sniper should slip in the back way and plink his ass. Never a brave man and always paranoid, he added the extra guards to keep an eye on the original ones because they work for the Secret Service and he was always suspicious of anyone having secrets he wasn't in on.

He had good reason to be suspicious, too. Secret Service agents saw him as himself, a devious, mean-spirited man with an IQ lower than the minimum wage and no scruples whatsoever. When asked if they'd take a bullet for the president they gave the stock answer and said yes but they always crossed their fingers. The general consensus among agents was that should any shooting erupt they'd seize the opportunity and shoot the smirking asshole themselves.

By the way, some may feel it's inappropriate to call the President of the United States an asshole but he and his asshole vice-president started it when they called a reporter an asshole on national TV. Sauce for the goose and all that, you know.

As for the population as a whole, most were unconcerned since the rebels still killed only politicians. It's true, though, that people began avoiding politicians for fear of being caught in the crossfire when the shooting started. Where most congressional offices normally had a steady stream of shady people with shifty eyes and sinister bearings going and coming, recent events had reduced the streams to mere trickles. No one wanted to be in the office when the rebels showed up to shoot the bastard and end up an innocent victim.

Naturally, this loss of business was costly for the pols. Studies show the average congressperson earns

$165,000 in salary and six times as much in bribes, kickbacks, assorted scams, and outright theft. As a result of the drop-off in their cash flow, many of them were reduced to living on their salaries and obeying the law.

Alas, it proved too much for several of them. There were eleven suicides in the first weeks of the money drought and three other attempts that failed because the saps were unable to tie a decent knot. Many others lost their multi-million dollar estates and had to move to homes costing as little as $500,000 and suffered great humiliation and disgrace. Mercedes limos were swapped for Honda Civics, private schools for public, $10 cigars for cigarillos, cruises for backyard barbecues. Many wondered if the entire government might collapse unless graft and corruption were quickly restored.

There were compensating factors that made the whole mess less discouraging and somewhat easier to deal with if one lived in Europe, Asia, Africa, Australia, or the rest of the Western Hemisphere. Each new assassination was greeted with something bordering on glee. This was especially true in the Muslim world where everybody already hated us and saw our recent troubles as being wrought by Allah to punish the infidels.

Al Jazeera's ratings shot up like a new congressperson's bank account every time it ran pictures of another dead American politician. School children skylarked and burned American flags, schools closed for a holiday, block parties sprang up everywhere, Al Qaeda recruiting drives broke old records, and a grand time was had by all.

Everything considered it was not a good time for the Administration, our war effort, international relations, Fritz Kessler, or current members of Congress. It was a dandy time for everybody who hates us.

CHAPTER FIFTEEN

Meanwhile, things weren't going that well for Kessler. Scanlon was convinced he'd captured the criminal of the century and saved the nation from total destruction. He thought the Gray Eminence was in the same league with Hitler, Stalin, Pol Pot, Idi Amin, Richard Nixon, and other infamous murderers, pillagers, and thugs and the sooner hanged the better.

So he held Kessler incommunicado, allowing him to see no one including his lawyers, though this was a direct violation of his Constitutional rights. He was even denied writing paper or pens, radio and TV, reading material except for a Bible in what was essentially solitary confinement.

In fact, his only visitors were interrogating agents and the guy who brought his meals, a somber black man named Dennis who winked and indicated the camera in the ceiling with his eyes. They had Kessler on a limited diet of mostly unattractive comestibles but the clever waiter hid meatballs in the thin gruel-like soup and mixed tuna into the lettuce salad. Kessler made a mental note to reward his benefactor when the new order was established.

After the Spooner hit Scanlon was summarily summoned to the Director's office to explain what the hell was going on.

Scanlon entered and Director Slinker said, "What the hell's going on?"

Scanlon shrugged and then realized that wasn't

going to work as an answer so he tried again. "Uh, I mean, we don't really know, sir. We even had an SS man watching him…"

"We're using Nazis now?" Slinker said, alarmed.

"No, sir, that's Secret Service…"

Slinker harrumphed and scowled. "Where the hell was your SS man?"

"Uh, he was on his lunch break, sir."

"He was, was he?"

"Yes, sir. So, anyway, the Gray Eminence won't talk and he's the only person we know who's had any contact with the rebels. Without him we have no leads at all and…"

"The country falls to the rebels and we all have to get honest jobs."

"Oh, sir," Scanlon said, shocked. "I don't think it will ever come to that…"

But Slinker wasn't listening; he was thinking. "You know," he said thoughtfully, "the situation where a terrorist knows where an H-bomb is set to go off but he won't tell how to find it and save the city? Isn't that exactly what we have now? Kessler can tell us where that bomb is. I say send His Eminence to Israel!"

"Don't you mean Egypt, sir? We usually send people to Cairo and…"

"No, Isreal's got a special this month. I got a coupon."

"But, sir, won't that cause a stir when people find out we sent K to be tortured?"

"Oh, shit. The people. It's always about the goddamn people." He scowled and furrowed his brow and thought about the people but found it so unsettling he stopped doing it. "We could smuggle him out in a laundry cart, put him in a van, and get him out to the plane in the middle of the night. Who would know?"

"Everyone, sir. No one knows where rebels might be."

"Surely, you don't mean…!"

"Not in the Bureau, sir, but anywhere else and…"

"Hmm. Okay. A strategic maneuver. Swing into Operation FR."

"Uh, which one is that again, sir?"

"Operation FR. Be fair and reasonable."

"Oh, right, sir, that one. Sorry. It's been a dozen years since anybody used that one around here, is all."

"Kessler is an intelligent man. Maybe we can reach him with logic and common sense."

"Uh, sir, what agents did you have in mind for Operation FR? I don't know that we have anybody here with…"

"Jesus Christ, man, do I have to do everything myself? If you can't run the store I'll find somebody who can!"

"No problem, sir. I'll get right on it, sir! I'll personally choose the right man for the job. You can count on me, sir!"

With that he backed out of the room bowing and scraping as if leaving royalty. He would have curtsied if he knew how—or would that have been inappropriate?

In any case, the die was cast and Scanlon began setting the stage for Plan B. His first task was to find agents who possessed both logic and common sense.

There was a fair number of agents that understood logic well enough and could handle most syllogisms and some who were well stocked with common sense, but very few possessed of both qualities with the one most often missing being common sense.

Scanlon found that common sense is a misnomer; there is nothing common about it. Ph.D.s often lack it while high school dropouts can have it in abundance. The inept genius is a stereotype, a cliché. Absent-minded professors are a staple of literature, helpless old-timers who split the atom and map the universe and can't remember where they work. Often it turns out that they work for some bozo that dropped out in his freshman year and opened a lab in his garage.

With time running out, Scanlon decided to do the job himself. While he didn't know much about logic—he thought syllogism was something vaguely naughty—he had years of experience crossing intellectual swords with some of the best pros out there and he usually came up a winner. Of course, what he didn't realize was that Kessler had both logic and common sense in uncommonly large amounts and was leagues beyond him on any playing field.

Scanlon launched Operation FR that very afternoon when he went down to Kessler's subterranean cell at lunchtime just as Dennis was delivering the usual gruel.

"Good news, Mr. Kessler," he said with false exuberance. "You've been reclassified as a VIP criminal and are entitled to new quarters. I apologize for your confinement here; you'll be much more comfortable in your new surroundings."

Dennis slipped between Scanlon and Kessler's tray so he wouldn't peek under the lids and spot the delicacies hidden there instead of the institutional crap on the official menu.

Kessler eyed Scanlon suspiciously, as kindness by one's captors is always suspect. What is he up to? Is there a catch? A prelude to something sinister? Of course, he revealed none of this to Scanlon. The trick was to go along and sound him out, see where he was coming from and act accordingly. It was a game he knew well from years of matching wits with opposing counsel in hundreds of trials and it stood him in good stead now.

Scanlon stepped aside and gestured for Kessler to precede him from the cell without the usual handcuffs. Dennis watched them go then smiled broadly as he sat down and opened the covered dishes to reveal a fine meal fit for him.

Kessler was led into an elegant dining room that would have met with any king's approval. There were only six tables and they had museum-quality table wear at each place setting, sparkling crystal glistened in the light from Tiffany chandeliers, Persian carpets, silk drapes, fine linens everywhere.

It was a room seldom seen by outsiders; in fact, not often seen by most agents, as the head guys were afraid they might steal some of the crystal. The room was used by potentates, big shots in the crime business, important friends of the Bureau who could be useful to the Agency. South American dictators were frequent visitors as were certain international drug lords, Russian KGB people, torture equipment salesmen, et al.

Even Kessler was impressed. Clearly, someone with impeccable taste had done the decorating, most likely someone not connected with the Bureau. Waiters in white coats popped into view and seated them at a table set for two that overlooked much of the city.

Scanlon leaned in confidentially and said, "Uh, look, Mr. Kessler, uh, may I call you Fritz…?"

"No."

"Uh, as I was saying, uh, you're a man of the world, successful attorney, a man who understands the nuances of things…"

"What things?"

"Things like patriotism, love of country, duty, responsibility…"

"How do I know you won't put me back in that cell?"

"Uh, you don't."

He took up his menu. "That's what I thought so I'm going to eat before you change your mind. At least I'll get a decent meal out of it."

Scanlon waved a finger at him. "New rules, Mr. Kessler. You are now a VIP."

The food was first-rate, the conversation entertaining but filled with a sense of expectation, as Scanlon sought to gather information and Kessler sought to avoid giving any. It was a cat and mouse game with no certainty as to which was the cat and which the mouse.

They'd finished with lunch and were eyeing a dessert cart filled with stuff just invented fifteen minutes ago by Chef Boyardee when Scanlon tried a more direct approach.

"Off the record, Mr. Kessler," he said off-handedly, "but do you think the rebels can actually overthrow the government of the most powerful nation on the planet?"

"Apparently you do or I wouldn't be under arrest." He pointed to something on the cart he didn't recognize but that looked scrumptious. "I'll have one of those."

"No, I mean really. That's crazy. A few guys spread all over the country, no communication, no major weapons, no leadership…" He scooped up something that looked like a blue-ribbon winner at the Annual Gourmet Awards show in Las Vegas and lost his train of thought while mentally savoring the first bite of whatever it was.

"Revolutions always start with a few men our own included. Governments age and become corrupt; the people are abused and resent it. It happens all the time."

Both men took substantial bites from their desserts and neither spoke as wondrous tastes converged and exploded on their palates and caused spontaneous smiles to break out on both faces. It was, in fact, somewhat of a breakthrough moment, the first time either had shown another side of his self. Not any sort of epiphany but a glimmer of recognition brought about by sharing dessert in a pleasant social setting.

"I think this was a good idea," Scanlon said. "Not because you might tell us anything new but because I got a closer look at you as a person. I mean, it's obvious you're not the lunatic I thought you were in the beginning."

"It isn't lunacy to love your country so much that you'll fight for it."

"That's what I mean. I think armed rebellion is pretty nuts to start with, but at least the rebels aren't doing it for personal gain. It looks like they really believe in what they're doing."

"They're risking their lives; you must believe in something before you'll do that."

"Is that why you're risking your life?"

"My life isn't at risk but I strongly believe in this revolution at this time and place. Every once in a while it's just the right thing to do."

"Even if the rebels kill half of Congress?"

"Even if the rebels kill all of Congress."

"You could be arrested just for saying that, you know."

"I'm already under arrest. You can't arrest me twice at the same time."

Scanlon laughed. "It might even be unconstitutional like double jeopardy."

They'd worked their way through dessert by this time and the white coats reappeared with snifters of Napoleon brandy that cost more than the exquisite crystal glasses that held it. The coup de grace came in a humidor lined with Cohiba cigars from Cuba that were both among the best smokes in the world and totally illegal due to our embargo. Apparently, not only was smoking allowed in the VIP room but so was committing a crime under the watchful eyes of the F.B.I.

Kessler wasn't a regular smoker but he did enjoy

an occasional celebratory cigar under the right circumstances so he and Scanlon lit up and spent the next hour in friendly discourse about many things but nothing about rebels and rebellions. While both had agenda they enjoyed a truce if not a cessation of hostilities and ended with a better sense of where each was coming from.

With the lunch debris swept away, brandy glasses empty, cigars snuffed out in a crystal ashtray, and appetites sated they paused and looked at each other for a moment before Scanlon offered his hand and Kessler took it and both new there would be new rules between them henceforth.

"Thanks for the lunch, Jim," Kessler said.

"My pleasure, Fritz," he replied, and they exchanged almost imperceptible nods to seal an ethereal compact.

From then on the Bureau's attitude toward Kessler changed for the better. He was housed in a comfortable room on the third-floor complete with all the amenities and minus handcuffs or even locked doors. While still strongly suspected of complicity with the rebels, it was decided that a different approach might produce better results as it became clear that the Gray Eminence would not break under conventional interrogation.

As a result Kessler became more like a guest than prisoner. He ate in the staff dining room, enjoyed Napoleon brandy, had TV, a phone, and even a computer. Needless to say, all this was constantly monitored, recorded, analyzed by Bureau experts looking for the slightest clue that would either lead them to the rebels or connect Kessler with them in some evidentiary way. No phone call was placed without pre-approval, websites were screened as were all incoming calls, and many TV channels were blacked out including CNN and all news shows. Everyone understood the rules, of course, but then everyone knew the stakes involved.

Once Kessler was ensconced in his new quarters he called Bob at the Sentinel to announce his availability but Bob was still holed up at Colleen's so he got Pete, instead. Bob didn't want Scanlon to have his cell number but Pete knew it would be even worse to give Colleen's number since it would reveal his hideout. He chose the lesser of two evils and surrendered the cell number.

Kessler punched in the numbers. "Bob. Kessler here. How are you?"

"Holy smoke, it's you! I was getting worried. I hope you're not calling from Egypt?"

"No," Kessler said, laughing, "I'm still in Hoover's Palace. This place has better accommodations than most hotels. I may plead guilty and sign a long-term lease."

"No rubber hoses or vicious beatings?"

"Some minor inconveniences up front, but nothing worth alerting Geneva about. What I really miss is news. They've put a complete news blackout in effect so I have no way of knowing what's happening."

"More of the same. Did you hear about Rep. Spooner?"

"Spooner?"

"Yeah, from Sacramento. Killed the other day with an arrow."

"An arrow?"

"Yeah, it was at an Indian casino. Scared the shit out of everybody in the Beltway. The town's starting to look like Baghdad; everyone's wearing armor and helmets and sitting with their backs against the wall. The army has troops surrounding the Capitol, the White House, the Pentagon, and all the major monuments. The country is on a war footing."

"It won't help. There's a force in motion out there that will not be denied. The rebels have waded across the Rubicon and are headed for Washington and a whole new government and they can't be stopped."

"So, what's the next step?"

"A meeting before the full Congress—or what's left when the shooting's over. We need to address the rebels' demands before this thing will end."

"You can't do that in Hoover's Palace. Any chance of getting out?"

"I haven't checked with my attorneys. I haven't heard from them lately. I may have to rely on an appeal to public opinion to force a hearing. Maybe you can promote the idea in your column."

"I don't know, I'm walking a fine line now. Some folks think I'm favoring the rebels as it is and that could put my ass in a sling if I'm not careful. These guys have locked up a lot of innocent bystanders in the past and they will again."

"Just be a reporter, they haven't eliminated freedom of the press yet."

"Can you have visitors?"

"Visitors? I'm lucky to have a phone."

"Any chance you could duck out when they aren't

looking?"

"Yes, there is. My door isn't even locked. But that would be counter productive because I'd then be a fugitive on the lam and I couldn't represent my clients."

"Maybe that's why you're not locked up. They hope you'll make a run for it and somebody will shoot you."

"Do you think my own government could be that devious?"

"Are you kidding?"

Kessler laughed and it made both of them feel good. "I'm ever watchful, Bob. They'll have to get up early in the morning to take me unawares."

"If I ever need a good mouthpiece I'll give you a ring."

"Let's hope that doesn't happen."

Simultaneous hang-ups.

CHAPTER SIXTEEN

The action picked up appreciably a few days later when Bob raised the matter of Kessler's continued incarceration in his column and demanded to know what the feds and done with him. Had they mistreated him? Was it true they hired ex-Abu Gareib guards to watch him? Were dogs or nudity involved? Were there any Egyptians on the scene? Was he even alive?

Bob wasn't the only one interested in the answers to these questions. The piece produced a worldwide reaction evidenced by so many e-mails hitting the airwaves at once that Sen. Ted Stephens' famous "pipes" got clogged up and had to be plunged out and millions of them were lost forever.

Denied a chance to hear Kessler at his abbreviated press conference, people felt cheated and were pissed that the feds were doing it again. The resulting outpouring of mail, angry phone calls, pro-Gray Eminence editorials in foreign and even American newspapers, and talk show hosts demanding that the feds bring him forth and show him to the world struck no responsive chord at Hoover's Palace.

Director Slinker refused to be bullied. "I refuse to be bullied," he said. "Mr. Kessler is the leader of an armed rebellion and is a danger to the nation. He has had known contact with rebel forces, has encouraged them, supported them, and promoted their interests and is guilty of treason against the United States of America. The president has classified Mr. Kessler as an enemy combatant to be tried by a military tribunal in a secret place without recourse to an attorney. Once convicted his sentence will be carried out by a firing squad in a secret place and time. There will no appeal."

These words brought tears to the eyes of many former KGB inquisitors, retired Mossad squad members, Gulag chieftains, Christians, and Executive Office officials who remembered the halcyon days of yore when water boarding was regarded as child's play and confessions were obtained in minutes whether the guy was guilty or not. Alas, now this talk about Geneva Conventions, civil rights, and humanitarian crap was taking all the fun out of the interrogation profession.

In fact, this was borne out by the sharp drop in recruits in the world's principal torture centers. Cairo advertised for 6,000 apprentices and received only 3,000 queries. Bulgaria had positions for 2,800 interns and attracted just 900 applicants.

For most, torture had lost its allure, its charm. No longer a glamorous field, it began to attract lowlifes, usually homely and slow-witted but with thick necks. The pay fell off, too. Once paid handsome salaries, torturers went on hourly rates and lost their benefits. It was clear that without a return to those golden years when popes and kings supported torture we will soon be bereft of skilled practitioners and have to rely on amateurs who will likely botch things up and cause costly lawsuits for malpractice.

Kessler could take little comfort from this trend, however, since Cairo was still awash with qualified torturers working in our rendition program. Special squads under the direction of the Homeland Security czar prowled our streets kidnapping citizens identified as likely to be guilty of something and they're wrestled into unmarked cars, driven to obscure airfields, and flown to Cairo. Our agents tell them what they want the guy to confess, the renders set to work with a will, and presto! A signed confession is produced before lunch and all retire to a pleasant plaza to drink weak tea and chew a little kat.

So, he wouldn't be tortured, at least not yet. Having figured this out himself, Kessler bided his time and enjoyed the hospitality of Hoover's Palace.

Meanwhile, on the home front that evening Bob was in the kitchen cleaning up after dinner while Colleen worked in her office on her review of an upcoming Hilfiger collection. He closed a cupboard door, took off Colleen's apron, and started to put it down when he stopped and stared first at the apron and then at the sparkling kitchen. Horrified, he marched into Colleen's office.

"I quit!" he said.

She didn't look up. "You can't quit."

"What?"

"You owe for the rent. It's kind of like a 21st century debtors' prison. You can't go until the debt is paid. That's three grand a month."

"What?"

"Three grand." She swept the room with her hand. "All this luxury doesn't come cheap, you know."

"Bullshit. That's more than your mortgage payment."

"Yes, it is, but you get services that don't usually come with the average mortgage."

"Are you charging me for sex?"

"Yes, but it's my wholesale rate. You couldn't afford retail."

"Oh, yeah? Well, what if I just walk out right now?"

She turned and looked at him. "You won't do that because you like it here. It's cleaner than your place, better located, media free, and you have me." She smiled a knowing smile and crossed her excellent legs to expose vast reaches of first-rate thigh and discombobulated Bob entirely.

"Well," he said, eyes fixed on her thighs, "don't forget this is a temporary arrangement. Once the heat's off the Kid is moving on."

"Of course," she said. "Whoever said it was for life?"

Satisfied that he'd held his own and stood up for men everywhere, he went back to hang up Colleen's apron and gave a Stan Laurel nod to seal the deal.

The next afternoon Bob sneaked into the paper and took care of a number of things that had accumulated since he'd taken up shelter with Colleen. That done, he shopped around in his head for a new slant on things. While there was a lot going on as it was there wasn't much new stuff. What new element could he bring into play?

Then his eye caught a story in the newspaper lying open on his desk where the pope declared all other religions were wrong and salvation could only be found in the Catholic faith. This was somewhat controversial and drew dissenters from all the religions on Earth but that wasn't what interested Bob. No one had sought the views of the clergy on the rebellion and he resolved to do so.

A call to Cardinal McFoneés office produced an appointment with the Cardinal for the very next day. As a rule, it's easier to see a senator or governor than a Cardinal but having a column in the Sentinel can open doors that would remain tightly closed to an average sinner seeking guidance. The good Cardinal was eager to talk about anything that didn't involve wayward priests.

The next day Bob put on a tie and wore newly cleaned and pressed jeans to meet with His Excellency. The Cardinal's palace was situated on a street with other palaces but his was by far the most magnificent. Set on six acres and surrounded by gardens filled with exotic flowers, a score of different kinds of trees, a waterfall and pond frequented by ducks, and statuary stolen from a dozen countries and historic periods, it was elegance and taste of the very highest order.

The whole was so spectacular and marvelous that Bob actually thought he might abandon Satan and throw in with Jesus again but he didn't. Some things are just not worth it. A liveried butler met Bob at the door and led him into a foyer so big it had an echo. A grand staircase soared upward and carried one's spirit with it to…what? Heaven or merely an upper-floor?

They met in the library and sat in Spanish leather easy chairs so much like soft butter that Bob kept sliding out of his. The Cardinal was a wizened little guy with a beak curved like a small scimitar and cheeks straight from Renoir's palette. He wore the traditional red robes of a Prince of the Church with a beanie sans propeller on his baldpate. While he moved his tiny hands in elegant little passes as he spoke and tried to appear magisterial, he still looked more like a bookkeeper than a potentate.

Bob got right down to business.

"What's the Church's position on the rebellion going on today?"

"Oh, we're against it, of course. Rebellions always turn out badly for one side or the other and we don't like the odds. Fifty-fifty? W.C. Fields would never approve."

"So, who's the sucker here?"

"Your opponent. It's always wise to bet with suckers."

Bob was impressed. "Jesus Christ," he said, "no wonder you guys have been around so long!"

His Highness nodded modestly. "Yes, we've survived not only because we were able to outwit others, but because we had the good sense to incorporate in 303 AD and, since corporations never die, neither does the Catholic Church."

"That's the year that marked the end of the Age of Martyrs, isn't it?

"Yes. It was a banner year for us. We had a monopoly on God for the next twelve centuries until…"

The Prince stopped and scowled fiercely.

"Until Luther came along and queered your act."

"And you ask the Church's views on rebels?"

"So, what would you do with our rebels?"

"Public immolation. It's both entertaining and informative. You could televise it on CNN and send a message to would-be rebels everywhere. School children could file by and throw faggots on the fire…"

"What? You want to burn gay people?"

"Faggots as in bundles of sticks."

"Oh, right. But do you think it's appropriate for kids to help set a guy afire?"

"Certainly. Children are very impressionable. I assure you not one of them would ever forget the experience."

"Unfortunately, you're probably right."

Suddenly, Bob looked up and saw a teacart replete with all the fixings for an old-fashioned British high tea. The comestibles had appeared almost as if by magic and he sneaked a look around to see if there might be the odd angel or spirit loitering nearby.

"Do have some tea," His Majesty said. "And try the crumpets; I ordered them myself."

Bob did so and conversation lagged while both laid waste to everything on the cart that was edible. One would have expected the Cardinal to be an abstemious man judging from his stature, but he was a real trencherman who doubtless had the metabolism of a shrew on speed and never gained an ounce.

Once the edibles were gone Bob figured it was time for him to go so he proceeded to wrap things up.

"If I may, Your Holiness, can I get your views on a few quick questions?"

"Of course."

"What's the Church's position on universal health care?"

"Unnecessary. God will look after you."

"Do you have health care?"

"What?"

"Separation of church and state?"

"The Devil's work. The Founding Fathers were under the influence of Satan."

"Labor unions?"

"Unnecessary. Workers should trust their employers to be fair with them."

"Laws to make it harder for poor people to file bankruptcy?"

"Perfectly reasonable. People should pay their just debts. There are too many deadbeats in this country."

Bob snapped his notebook shut to announce the end of the interview and prepared to go.

"I want to thank you for seeing me, Your Worship," he said. "My readers will be interested to learn the views of the Church on this matter and you may even influence the thinking of some government officials— even if autos-da-fé are probably illegal."

"We're a traditional organization, Mr. Ingersoll. Most of our thinking is rooted in the Middle Ages when life was simpler and most people couldn't read. Nowadays, we have to scramble to keep home and hearth together and meet the challenges of modern times."

"You're doing a bang-up job, sir. I'll pass your modern version of autos-da-fé along to the Administration. I'm sure that bunch will love it."

"Will you want a photograph?" He started searching through drawers. "I have one here somewhere…"

"No, that's okay, Your Kingship, I don't use pictures with my column."

"Yes, all right." He seemed disappointed but that was okay since Bob was also disappointed.

Bob left but didn't use any of the interview in his

column. He did, though, keep his word and forwarded the Royal suggestion re burning rebels for fun and profit. He was not surprised to receive a reply from the White House that thanked him for his input and tried to sell him a ticket to a $1,000 a plate fundraiser.

CHAPTER SEVENTEEN

The pressure continued to mount both at home and around the globe as Kessler remained incommunicado, the rebels uncaught, the government apparently inept, and the world watching in breathless wonder and expectation. What would the government do? Why is Kessler hidden away? What will be the rebels' next move? Will the rebellion be successful? Why can't the feds catch the rebels? What ever happened to Judge Crater? What do the American people think about the rebellion?

The most striking result of our rebellion was in the Muslim world. Jihads were cancelled and the fighters sent home because there was no need for them, as the Western devils were destroying themselves. Recruiting drives for suicide martyrs were scaled down, Hamas and Hezbollah signed a truce, and bomb sales fell off perceptibly. Al Jazeera did its part by carrying a running account of news from the States with each new assassination and impaneled experts to discuss every nuance of the fall of American imperialism and the triumph of Allah.

In effect, the Muslim holy war against the West was put on hold. People came out of their mostly battered homes and thanked Allah for punishing the Devil's disciples in Washington, a sentiment shared by most Americans and everybody else. In fact, many felt the rebellion was a good thing because it shut down the war on terror and gave us a chance to fight the enemy here where we can find them rather than over there where we can't. If nothing else it saved us a lot of the money we were currently spending to ship everything to the Middle East, especially with the cost of gas these days.

Of course, a war is a war and there was still Iraq. The enemy was so entranced at what was happening in America that they reduced their bomb attacks by 20% and promised to reduce them by 2% more for every new assassination until they saw who won over here.

Was this a humanitarian gesture or a clever plan to encourage American rebels to shoot pols at a quicker pace? Any patriot who knew in his heart that the war was unnecessary and evil might easily be tempted to knock of a passing senator if he could save American lives in Iraq. You might even do it yourself.

So, just days after Spooner's demise, sweeping changes had occurred worldwide and the rebellion was hardly underway. It struck a nerve everywhere and focused attention on a changing universe where Third World countries were turning into place finishers while others moved into show spots with all the rest moving up a notch. Somebody was making new rules, better ones aimed at making everybody's life a little richer, longer, happier.

Just when everybody was settled into a kind of routine, then, a mini-riot broke out in Los Angeles when an angry mob stormed a local medical marijuana dispensary and made off with its entire stock of herbs. Some claim the mob shouted, "Free the Gray Eminence!" as they rushed the place to give a political overtone to the whole affair, but others felt the shibboleth was merely to conceal their real purpose, which was to get some free smoke.

In either case, both things happened. The rioters got their smoke and Kessler got a boost in his ratings, as news of the riots spread and small but noisy riots broke out in half-a-dozen cities demanding he be brought out into the light or else. The press was thrilled to have a fresh angle and the TV people were beside themselves with footage they could run for days as they beat the story into media mush.

Naturally, Bob wrote of the riots himself and took the mob's side when he excoriated the Administration for persisting in its crypto-fascist government and demanded they produce the Gray Eminence and address the issues before the American people. Mail opposing his position dwindled to a trickle as even the least bright among us came to realize the country was run by crooks, tyrants, warmongers, plutocrats, and traitors and they had to be stopped.

All of the answers rested with Fritz Kessler and a curious nation and world wanted to know.

The boys at the Bureau were alarmed at the riots, of course. The last thing Director Slinker wanted was to give Kessler a forum, and this was made clear to him by White House big shots. Kessler would be held incommunicado until they hanged his ass, after which he would be free to give interviews or even write a book. Slinker's job was not made easier by rioting mobs and he was pissed.

Scanlon advanced on the Director's desk warily, as one might approach a coiled cobra, while Slinker watched Scanlon as the cobra might eyeball potential prey or danger. There was little doubt as to which was cobra and which prey.

"What about these goddamn riots, Scanlon? What the hell's going on?"

"We don't know, sir. They're spontaneous. They just pop up all of a sudden."

"Listen, it's your job to know what's going on. Find out. Order every office to put some men on these riots. Get the local cops to make some arrests. Find out who's in charge, names of participants, check 'em for priors. The goddamn rebels are behind this and I want the bastards caught."

"Yes, sir. I'll get right on it."

And he did. Subsequent riots produced many arrests and background checks and didn't catch a single crook. All rioters were young people from good families with high GPAs in school and motivated by a strong desire for better and cleaner government. There wasn't a verifiable rebel in the lot, no organization to speak of, no leaders, no profit motive, no personal injuries involved.

In general, these were some of the most controlled and disciplined public disturbances ever and hard to attack with the usual propaganda tools. Not even the Swift Boat Veterans for Truth could find fault with the rioters and they're the ones that torpedoed Kerry with their lying bullshit in '04.

The result was that unrest mounted and so did peoples' impatience. The White House was alarmed and by now fearful that the peasants might storm the Oval Office and massacre every politico in sight and the rest when they caught them. The president even had work started on an escape tunnel that would lead to a sanctuary somewhere in Virginia should rebels attack.

But there was more to come. Bob had taken to going out more now that people had had time to adjust to things and were less freaked out by it all. He even went back to his condo and was surprised to see the media had pulled out and moved on. He entered the building and his apartment to find it in somewhat better shape than when he left it thanks to Colleen's house cleaning efforts when she stopped by for his things earlier.

He cleaned out the fridge and threw away dishes that looked inedible, i.e., almost everything. Sunlight filtered through shutters, Vivaldi filled the room, and smoke eddied and drifted in the still air as he stretched out in his easy chair and sipped steaming cinnamon-flavored arabica coffee from his very own mug and he was at peace with the world. It was true; there is no place like home.

But something was missing. Colleen. There was nobody to talk to here. The place needed a good scrubbing, the furnishings weren't suitably coordinated, and he kept his preferred slick, modern look only by turning the closets into commercial storage lockers for professional pack rats. And he had nobody to talk to.

In the end he decided not to tell Colleen just yet that his own place was available again. Instead, he rationalized that since it was closer to work he'd stay at her place for the time being. So he locked up and headed for his new temporary home with Colleen.

What he didn't know, though, was that Colleen had been by his place three days ago and found the media no longer in attendance. On her part she didn't bother to tell him and decided to play out the game. Who could tell what fate may have in store for them? And why not help it decide which way things should go?

In any case, the pace picked up that evening. Colleen had an interview with Donna Karan and Bob just wanted to get out of the house so he donned dark glasses and floppy hat and went out on the town as a regular citizen.

He walked briskly for six blocks due east and returned the same way much refreshed. It wasn't much but it felt good to move his limbs for something besides readjusting his position in an easy chair. He'd passed a pleasant restaurant patio on the way and stopped on the return trip for a glass of chilled Riesling to steady his nerves.

He took a second sip and found he'd suddenly acquired a guest. A man wearing a T-shirt and khakis pulled out the chair opposite him and sat down on it. He was short but not small with a bodybuilder's arms and bearing. He was not smiling.

"Good evening," he said.

"Good evening."

"I have an item for tomorrow's column," he said in a flat monotone. "Release the Gray Eminence within seventy-two hours or there will be renewed attacks by rebel forces. A specific number of targets will be hit and there will be no further discussion of terms until that number is reached. We start counting at noon."

"And you are?"

"A messenger."

"So we're not supposed to kill you?"

He smiled. "No one shoots the messenger anymore."

"How do I know that you know?"

"You don't but you will in seventy-two hours."

"Do you know Kessler?"

"Yes, but he doesn't know me. I heard him speak once."

"You're a supporter of his?"

"I'm an American citizen trying to save my country from traitors and crooks. I won't stop—we won't stop—until we get a new government, one run by people who can read and will respect our Constitution. The American people lost more rights in the last few years than your average death row inmate and we aim to take 'em back."

"With guns?"

"Is there another way?"

"The electoral process?"

He shook his head. "Not this time." He stood up to go.

"Wait. Who told you about this? Was it Kessler? Is he running this thing?"

But the man was done talking and moved off without a backward glance. Bob watched him go and wasn't sure if he had a terrific scoop or if the guy was a total phony. Who was running the rebellion? How could Kessler run it from Hoover's Palace? Was there a second Gray Eminence, one who was actually running the show?

Bob finished his wine and went home to lay it on Colleen and get her slant on it but she was still out so he took a few hits on a roach and wrote the column just to see what it would look like. He told himself it was just for practice but knew he'd love it and he did.

He told of the man's warning and of their conversation, but he was careful to remind his readers that it hadn't been verified because there was nobody who could do that. It gave him some wriggle room if it was a hoax or just wrong, yet still counted as a scoop of major proportions if it turned out to be true. He showed it to Colleen when she came home and asked her opinion even though he'd decided it was first-class reporting and would print it.

She concurred but started on a different point. "This guy. He knows you and pops up out of nowhere with a tip. He's obviously got a connection with the rebels and may even be one of the killers. How safe is that? Could someone decide to kill you? Is it time for you to hand the story over to Pete?"

"Hey, I'm in no danger. The rebels won't kill me; I tell their story for 'em. I think they might even be right and I say so. There's a better chance the feds might shoot me than…"

Colleen put a hand to her mouth with a new fear. "Oh, my God! I never thought of that! Scanlon could shoot you..!"

"Scanlon? Naw, they'd import a hit squad from overseas. Probably the Mossad, as they're the most experienced. I'm safe as long as I don't spot a bunch of guys coming after me with a blonde transvestite in the lead."

"I hope you're right," she said, a distinct lack of conviction evident in her voice.

"Hey, what about the column? How's it look?"

"I like it. It's dramatic; it's even got a deadline, one that really is a deadline. Will they let Kessler have his press conference? Will the shooting start in seventy-two hours if they don't?"

"And there's the mystery angle, too. Who is the informant? Is he the headman himself? Is he one of the actual killers? It's a new genre, a mystery thriller in a newspaper column complete with heavies and good guys and a cast of millions."

"It's good, Bob. I only hope not too good."

"Say, you're worried about me, aren't you? That's not in the deal. I'm just a renter, nobody worries about renters."

"The rent is what I'm worried about. You and I are just ships in the night."

"That's better. Say, how'd the interview go? Did Donna give you any sample dresses?"

Colleen recounted the details of her meeting with the famed designer for the next half-hour and both were caught up in her story, she in the telling and he in listening. Though neither would admit it an air of domesticity settled around them and introduced a new element into their relationship that was turning it into something else almost unbeknownst to either of them.

CHAPTER EIGHTEEN

Bob's column ran as written and his phone rang twenty minutes after the papers hit the street.

"Ingersoll…"

"You bastard! I oughta charge your ass with war crimes…!"

"Hey, that's no way to talk to a citizen…"

"You got the info last night and decided to share it with us the next day…!"

"So? The three-day deadline doesn't start until noon."

There was a pause and Bob thought he heard a sigh. "Bob, do you know what obstruction of justice is?"

"Sure, it's what the president did in the Libby case."

"Or withholding evidence?"

"What evidence? Everybody knows you don't have any evidence. You said so yourself. All I had was an anonymous tip and that's not evidence."

"Bob, let me say this again. I'm officially ordering you to report any contact with the rebels to me immediately. Any mail, phone calls, tips, informers, 'Net postings, anything at all. I don't mean the next day or after lunch. If you do not I will bring charges against you that would confound Judge Learned Hand. Is that clear?"

"Look, Scanlon, I'm not trying to screw you up. I figured it didn't matter when I told you since you can't do anything about it, anyway. But okay, let's do it your way. If I get anything I'll let you know soonest. How's that?"

"Better. Now, what else can you tell me about the

guy?"

"Nothing. It's all in the column. He left without saying goodbye. I never saw him before. He looked fit, buzz cut, no scars or tattoos."

"Did he get in a car?"

"Not that I saw."

"No one with him? Maybe waiting for him down the block?"

"Nope."

"Okay. No more secrets."

"Hey, how's Kessler? Can I see him?"

"Uh, I don't know. Maybe."

"Maybe? I take that for a yes."

"I'll let you know. Remember, call."

"Right."

The hang-ups occurred in unison and Bob did the Laurel nod again for emphasis.

Bob punched in attorney Kelley's number to apprise him of the latest developments. The attorney had filed enough papers in Kessler's behalf to free the Manson family and expected to hear something in six or eight months. In the meantime, he was to meet with Kessler that afternoon to review his case but was told in advance he would remain incommunicado to the world.

It was apparent to Bob that the legal process would never save Kessler. The feds reached into their own Manual and came out with the reliable Fall Guy bit. Kessler filled the role of the blamed one, the framed one, even, and it mattered not a whit if he was guilty or innocent. Only a miracle could save him from the maws of injustice and that meant he was screwed, as miracles are so rare today that the franchise at Lourdes has filed for bankruptcy.

The president took a bold stand and said he'd never give in to the rebels no matter how many congresspersons they murdered. His audience cheered and he strutted like a popinjay in the belief they were cheering him, but they actually just liked the idea of shooting more politicians.

As for the intended targets, most were not amused. Some alluded to ducks in a shooting gallery but the more perspicacious among them chose our troops in Humvees in Iraq for an analogy. The president would defy the rebels from the Oval Office with the same intrepid courage he displayed in ordering his plane to fly to Nebraska on 9/11 to, as he himself put it, "…get out of harm's way." He thought our representatives expendable—and they are, of course.

The three days went by in a metaphysical trice and an entire nation and much of the world waited anxiously for the first politician to drop dead. Some with an entrepreneurial bent even started office pools on the dates assassinations would occur, the names of the victims, and so on. Websites sprang up everywhere and posted ticking clocks, sightings of pols to alert assassins to target availability, voting records of those most deserving to be shot first, where to buy guns and bullets, and similar information.

They didn't have long to wait. It happened that the very next day three GOP House members were on their way to conspire with agents from a defense contractor to sell sensitive satellite equipment to China so they could make better submarines with which to sink our ships when they had an accident. It seems they were hightailing it on a freeway through some very scenic mountains in

California when their car was sideswiped and knocked ass over applecart off a high cliff. Someone remarked that the cliff provided a splendid view they might have enjoyed on their way down. There were no survivors and somewhere somebody collected on an office pool.

The car that hit them was found further along the highway but it had been stolen and offered no clues whatsoever. A fellow insurgent apparently picked the driver up and what was clearly a well-planned attack was carried off without a hitch.

The feds swarmed on the scene en masse, spirited the damaged car away, and ordered a blackout on the details. What information they gave to the media implied that it had been an accident but the whole world scoffed as one and the force of the expended air blew a butterfly into the Indian Ocean and may have prevented a hurricane.

The politicians knew it was no accident, too, and fourteen of them submitted their resignations that very afternoon. Six of them bore foreign postmarks. Those that didn't flee took to the mattresses, so to speak. They disappeared so quickly and completely that many suspected David Copperfield might be involved. It made for an eerie Capitol with steps sounding hollowly in the empty halls, parking lots mostly vacant, and wary guards eyeing the odd lost tourist suspiciously.

All agreed later that the total lack of legislation during this time had a salubrious effect on the country, as it meant corruption and graft were reduced and no bridges were built to nowhere. One of the assholes infamous for promoting earmarks was Rep. Jack Murray (D-PA). He had a conniption fit, of course, since he lost out on hundreds of earmarks he'd lined up to bamboozle the public and enrich his cronies and the poor bastard went into cataleptic shock and remained frozen with outstretched hands grasping at empty air. It was a pathetic sight and sad but deserved, as he was a truly monumental asshole.

That wasn't all. The nation had barely adjusted to these deaths when two of their colleagues joined them on that dusty road. Higby and Freeman of the GOP and New Jersey were so crooked they were denied forgiveness by their priest after confession and ordered never to come back again. The shocked priest later said he'd once heard confession by Idi Amin and these guys made him look like a humanitarian in comparison.

Anyway, the duo was in cahoots with South American drug lords in an elaborate money-laundering scheme that netted them millions. Actually, it was their work on the House Committee on Crime and Drugs that first piqued their interest and led to the Suarez gang, an international drug smuggling operation that flooded the world with the dread marijuana bush.

An unintended consequence of all this pot brought enlightenment and understanding to untold millions and scared the bejabbers out of politicians everywhere. As vampires to light, so are politicians to intelligent voters. Nothing is more threatening than a voter who can think and, therefore, recognize demagoguery. As a result, the pols refuse to legalize the herb and hire drug czars to demonize the stuff with fried eggs and bullshit.

So Higby and Freeman rendezvoused with their fellow conspirators and were promptly shot dead. It seems the rebels knew of the deal and convinced the other side to drop out; it was the sort of arrangement the

Godfather might have made where the options are few. It also happened that the rebels ended up with a vast amount of cash intended to cement the deal. Investigators never learned of the money so there was no follow-up and it went to Doctors Without Borders, one of Kessler's favorite charities.

That made five new corpses three days after the deadline with an undisclosed number of politicians slated to accompany them into Valhalla. Four more pols resigned, six went into rehab, and forty-two announced they wouldn't run again. One even disguised himself as a penitent, joined the Trappist monks, and took a vow of silence to convince any potential assassins that he was reformed and no longer deserved killing. His ploy didn't work, though, as his fellow monks discovered his true identity and they beat him to death.

By this time the rebellion had ceased to amuse folks as more of them came to understand the reality of things. While the wholesale slaughter of politicians is obviously entertaining on its face, it is less so when the numbers head for double digits. When the money launderers died, for example, the polls showed a drop in approval ratings from 86% to 82%. Although it wasn't reported, the poll also showed that the 10% who disapproved of shooting politicians favored public whippings with the number of lashes averaging 100. The remaining 8% were idiots who didn't understand the question.

The president took a keener interest when a pundit remarked that no one was safe, not even the commander-in-chief himself. When he read that comment he ordered Air Force One readied for a quick trip to Nebraska but was dissuaded when aides suggested people might see it for what it really was, i.e., a cowardly flight to safety.

Instead, he called for the complete mobilization of all forces including veterans from WWII, Korea, and Vietnam as well as all retired military personnel, reserves, and every National Guard unit not already in Iraq. When told these forces would be insufficient he broke his promise never to do so and called for a draft to get the required troops. It would be an all-out war against the rebels, no quarter asked or given, no cost too great. All would make sacrifices; none would be spared.

Then he sneaked out in the dead of night and scuttled off to his so-called ranch sans horses, cattle, or any signs of agriculture.

And so it went for the next three weeks during which six senators, eight representatives, two federal judges, and an Undersecretary of State were sent off to perdition with alarm rising on each new report. Even more alarming was the fact that an additional thirty-one state and local politicians had been shot, stabbed, or run over in six states. It was clear that the rebellion was spreading when abused citizens struck out at the pols nearer to home and on such a wide front.

On the twenty-eighth day Bob got another letter. Its single sheet said, "It's time to talk. Where and when?"

As promised, Bob called Scanlon and he hurried over to secure the evidence.

Scanlon read the letter and looked up. Bob shrugged and said, "I guess they met their quota."

"What quota?"

"They said they'd kill a specific number if the feds didn't agree to parley. Now they're ready to talk so…"

Scanlon heaved a heavy sigh and said, "You know

what? I think it's time we did just that. I mean, we haven't got a goddamn clue on any of this. We have no evidence, suspects, or witnesses. No murder weapons. Nothing."

"Why not give them a little more time? If we say no they'll kill some more politicians, maybe eventually all of them, and then we can parley."

Scanlon shook his head. "I've got a better idea. We meet with the rebels, grab 'em and send 'em off to Cairo, torture 'em to find out who their leaders are, and arrest 'em. A series of public executions and we win."

"Run that by your boss. If he likes it he's a fool. These guys are in this thing to win; if there are any executions it's likely they'll be the ones tying the knots."

"Shit," Scanlon said. He turned and left the room, shoulders drooping and a shuffle in his walk, eyes downcast. Bob watched him go and saw a defeated man on his way to his own virtual execution.

Scanlon did make his report, Director Slinker duly informed his superiors, and the word finally arrived at the Oval Office where it was forwarded to the president at his ranch. The president flatly refused to meet with the rebels and tore the message to pieces.

The following night a sniper killed the Vice President of the United States as he returned home from a covert meeting with Halliburton officials about a new series of no-bid contracts worth billions to them and millions to him. Some witnesses claimed they heard a sardonic laugh as the veep fell; others thought it was the wind but there was no wind that night.

The world reacted by declaring an international holiday with picnics, fireworks, parades, speeches, and prizes. Taliban fighters came down from the hills and cavorted with their Afghanistan foes, prisons emptied out political prisoners, people danced in the streets, and Satan rubbed his hands in anticipatory glee as the down escalator—there is no up escalator—carried its cargo to Dante's lowest level.

The French closed the entire country and everybody celebrated for a week straight, the delighted Germans marked the occasion by expelling 10,000 Muslims for unruly behavior, and England hanged Tony Blair in effigy while a nation cheered. It was a memorable moment that would be celebrated for decades in lands near and far. Justice had triumphed, though somewhat tardily, and the evil bastard was dead.

The veep's funeral was held in the National Cathedral and everyone agreed it was pathetic. All of his friends attended and there was some confusion when both showed up in the section reserved for friends and there was but one seat set aside. It worked out, though, because there were lots of seats available elsewhere since most were empty. Even some of the family stayed away and one showed up wearing a disguise.

Inasmuch as the vicar had taken a sacred vow not to lie, he assigned the elegy to an atheist friend who hadn't taken such a vow and could therefore lie with impunity. That brave soul struggled manfully but the words clogged up his throat and blocked his windpipe and refused to leave his mouth. In the end a doctor had to perform an emergency tracheotomy on the altar to dislodge the debris and everybody went home satisfied that they'd done their duty.

They trucked the veep's remains off in the direction of the city dump while dozens lined the streets and pelted the hearse with catcalls and insults. It was a fitting tribute to one of the grandest assholes ever to trod the Earth.

After the veep's death the rebels' message finally registered with the Administration: the president agreed to meet with their leaders. Bob was at his desk when the call came in.

"Ingersoll."

"Ah, yes, Mr. Ingersoll. My name is Bill Conley. I'm with State Department. The president has agreed to meet with the rebel faction and would like you to post that in your column. They may specify the time and place. All participants will be granted immunity from arrest during the negotiations. Have them contact you with their reply."

"What about Kessler?"

"The president will order his release in the morning."

"You've just made my year, Mr. Conley."

"Yes, I imagine I have," he said dryly.

The line went dead and Bob grinned broadly and shot a clenched fist into the air. It was a homerun ball, bases loaded, everybody scored. Four zip. A shutout. The Pulitzer was as good as his.

Bob told the editor and nobody else for fear a leak would cost them a scoop worth two Pulitzers and a lot more. He wrote the column before he went home and left it with Pete who actually put it in his office safe lest the cleaning crew find it and bollocks up the whole operation.

Then Bob called Scanlon with the news.

"Yes?"

"I thought you'd like to know. The president has agreed to meet with the rebels. I just got a call from Bill

Conley at State. He says Kessler will be released in the morning."

"You're kidding!"

"Nope, it's straight from the horse's mouth. They'll schedule a date and the rebels will get their day in court."

"Holy shit!"

"Yeah, who would've thought it? Listen, we're breaking the story tomorrow. Do me a favor. Sit on this until morning. It'll be the biggest story ever and the Sentinel has earned the right to the scoop."

"Shit."

"Okay? You'll hold the story?"

Scanlon sighed audibly and Bob could almost see him chewing his lip.

"Sure, why not?"

"You're a pal, Scanlon."

Bob hung up and grinned a wide grin that would put a Cheshire cat in the shade. He headed for Colleen's office on the way out to share the good news and looked forward to that with pleasure. Mark Twain once remarked that joy must be shared while grief can be handled alone and Bob saw much truth in it as he approached her office.

She looked up as he entered and she instantly knew something was up because he beamed like a beacon and wore the air of a man well pleased with himself.

"Guess what?" he said.

"You just won a Pulitzer."

Bob was astounded. "Jesus Christ, who told you?"

"You mean you really did win a Pulitzer?"

"Well, not exactly, but I will."

"You got a big break in the story?"

"I sure did but I can't talk about it. Let's go to dinner. I'll even pay."

"Gee, a free dinner."

"Any restaurant. Cost is no object."

"Wow, you are on a roll!"

"We're on a roll. Come on, get your coat."

Colleen did as told and silently thought how nice it sounded to be on Bob's roll with him. Joy really is better shared.

They ate at 1789 on 36th street in Georgetown and both chose the most expensive meals on the menu with a first-rate wine as a chaser. The bill was a formidable one that Bob was careful to add to his expense account, a move detected by the ever-vigilant Colleen when he demanded a copy of the receipt.

"So much for an expensive celebratory dinner," she said wryly.

"Hey, it's the least the Sentinel can do for their ace reporter. Besides, they'll owe me a huge raise and I'm just collecting some of it early."

"I suppose I'll still be required to pay for part of it."

"I was hoping you would."

So they went home and made passionate love and Bob blabbed the whole story to Colleen because sensuous living and several hits of aromatic herb saved for just such an occasion weakened his resolve and loosened his tongue. Still, he felt safe enough since Colleen would not leave his side until morning and hence couldn't inadvertently sink his journalistic ship with a slip of the tongue.

Meanwhile, after Bob's call Scanlon checked with State to confirm Kessler's upcoming release and called on

Director Slinker to fill him in on the latest news.

"It's a goddamn mistake!" the headman exclaimed, smashing an imaginary somebody or something with a fist slashing the air. "You can't negotiate with traitors! How can you trust murdering thugs? They should be hunted down and shot like mad dogs, by God!"

"Yes, sir."

Slinker got a crafty look in his eye. "What if Kessler tried to escape? Could you shoot him?"

"Kessler won't try to escape, sir."

"But if he did you could shoot him, right?"

"I could, yes, but I could stop him without shooting him."

Slinker scowled. "You don't want to shoot the bastard, do you?"

"I'd rather not, sir."

He scowled some more. "You'll never be the Director of the Bureau, Scanlon. Do you know that?"

"Yes, sir."

"Okay, let the asshole go, but I want him followed 24/7. Find out who he meets, where and when. Bug his briefcase. Record every call. Report to me every day. Got that?"

"Yes, sir."

Ten minutes later Scanlon knocked on Kessler's door. "Yes?"

Scanlon entered and said, "Good news, Fritz. You're a free man."

"I am?"

"Well, you will be in the morning. The president caved. Your pals demanded a meeting and he said yes. They also demanded that you be released so you can act as their representative so you're sprung as of tomorrow morning."

"This is an unexpected turn of events, and not all that welcome. I was beginning to like it here."

"Don't make me evict you forcibly now."

"Oh, no. It's not that pleasant here."

An agent entered with Kessler's personal effects including a single suitcase and his briefcase. He put them on the bed and left.

"They're setting up a hearing. Bi-partisan. You're to explain your clients' position and negotiate for them."

Kessler looked at Scanlon. "It's been a long time coming, Jim. Too long."

Scanlon said nothing but hoped Kessler wouldn't find the bugs. It would nip a budding friendship in the bud.

The second act was about to unfold.

CHAPTER NINETEEN

The next morning Bob got to work early to await the explosion he knew was coming and he didn't have long to wait. The news spread like wildfire as it swept the city and then the rest of the country on TV, radio, phone lines, text messages, e-mail and smoke signals sent by Indians in lost New Mexico valleys where satellite TV feeds had misfired. America was at war with itself and was looking for a modern version of the Appomattox Courthouse to sort things out.

Attorney Kelley called for an update and to be sure he was included in any plans for his client to undergo questioning. Every media outlet in America called, wired, e-mailed Bob to appear with them or at least give them some quote they could offer to their clamoring audiences. He took none of their supplications.

At nine a.m. sharp Kessler strode from Hoover's Palace just like any other tourist, hailed a cab, and rode off into the bright sunlight. An unmarked police car followed, its occupants stern faced and all business.

He set himself up with a fleet of rooms in the Melrose Hotel and opened for business. He called Bob to arrange a quick press conference both to present himself to the world and to let people know that the fight for a new America was in fact succeeding. He understood that people need rallying points, something they can identify with: white horses, a charismatic leader, a flag, or even just a slogan. He would have to be that symbol.

Years in courtrooms influencing juries and fending off opposing counsel had instilled the confidence and skills required to take charge of a stage and reach people. The next few days and weeks would be the most important of his life and he was ready. It isn't too much to say that the fate of a nation and even much of the world hung in the balance.

No one really knew what Kessler looked like since his on-camera time was measured in seconds at his first press conference, so he was able to move about without attracting undue attention, at least for the nonce. He took a cab to the Sentinel building, marched inside unnoticed, and reached the city room before being recognized when Bob looked up and saw him standing near the entrance.

"Fritz!" he said. He sprang up and started for him.

"Ah, there you are," Kessler said. He offered his hand and they shook with the sort of enthusiasm usually found only in best friends meeting unexpectedly.

"Just like that! You're free!"

"It is sudden, isn't it? I knew they couldn't hold me forever but that wasn't all that comforting."

"It's all those dead politicians," Bob said. "The rebels got their attention when they started dropping like flies. The veep was the clincher."

"If nothing else the rebels have done yeoman work. They've rid the country of some of the worst of them; we'll be better off if that's all they do."

Bob checked the time. "The press conference is here at noon. There's a big conference room on the main floor. Its just media."

"Not too big. Good. We overreached last time."

Bob shrugged. "It would've worked if Boy Scout Scanlon hadn't played hero on us."

"No matter. We could meet in a closet as long as it's televised."

"We live in remarkable times, Fritz."

"Our children will live in even better times if we can make this work."

By this time word had spread that the Gray Eminence was in the city room and people began craning necks and looking in at the door and began to clog the hallway. As Bob and Kessler made their way to the elevator the crowd broke out in cheers and applauded them until the elevator doors closed.

Bob pushed the down button and said, "You will never have a completely private moment again, Fritz."

"Neither will you, Bob."

"Touché."

Their eyes met and they touched fists.

At five minutes to twelve Bob and Kessler stepped off the elevator in the lobby and straight into the Fourth Estate en masse—and these were just the ones who couldn't get in the conference room itself. When they managed to reach the entrance the people spilling out prevented their going in and for a moment it looked like they might call it off altogether.

Bob outflanked them, though. He led Kessler through the mob and past a sea of cameras, flashing lights, shouts, and struggling humanity and to a stairway leading to a storeroom beneath the conference room and thence to their goal.

Kessler grinned and shook his head. "Now I know

how Elvis felt."

"Elvis was never on a trip like this in his life. And neither was anybody else." He peered through a crack in the partly opened door and surveyed the room. "There must be a hundred people in there and everyone of 'em brought a camera and a microphone. And it's going out live."

"Good. Let's do it."

They stepped through the door and into a small open space behind a library table that was smothered with mikes and cords twisted into what looked like a 21st century version of the Gordian Knot. Unfortunately, Alexander was nowhere to be seen to sort this one out.

The event was so hurriedly assembled that there was no host, per se. Kessler moved to the table and stood gazing calmly at the assemblage. A striking figure, tall, slim with white hair, flinty blue eyes and handsome, he posed without seeming to pose, and left the entire world with a first impression that would forever be with each of them. Clearly, the Gray Eminence must have been a formidable opponent in court.

He sat down and blinked at the cameras as they flashed and sizzled and sent images flying worldwide at the speed of light. After a moment, he spoke in a relaxed, friendly manner without bombast or bluster.

"My name is Fritz Kessler. I am an attorney-at-law and I represent those individuals who are engaged in the overthrow of the illegitimate government of the United States of America." He paused just the right length of time. "The reasons for this action have been told you before. The current Administration has ignored the Constitution or, worse, rewritten it to support policies and acts detrimental to the nation and even the world.

"Civil rights long honored are taken from the people with arrogant Executive Orders, laws passed by Congress are emasculated by presidential signings indicating he will not enforce or obey them, politicians are wholly owned subsidiaries of special interest groups and no longer serve their constituents, illegal wars are fomented by lies, our reputation on the world stage savaged, ruined, scorned.

"For these and other reasons certain American citizens have taken it upon themselves to bring about change, to launch a new America based on the original model with rights restored to the people, honor and integrity to our government, and our old place restored as the leader of the free world and a friend to every person and nation on the planet."

He paused and took a sip of water from a bottle thoughtfully provided by an onlooker. "The government has agreed to meet with my clients in the next few days to hear the complaints of the people and suggestions for addressing them. I ask that you watch these hearings and judge for yourselves whether or not their complaints have merit. Thank you for coming."

The room erupted with a barrage of questions shouted in a single voice so loud that some in front were swayed by the force of the sound waves like a skyscraper in a high wind. Everyone leaned forward with outstretched mikes and cameras so that the throng moved as a single entity and only the table kept

Kessler and Bob from being pinned against the back wall with unlucky others.

Bob grabbed Kessler's arm and roughly jerked him toward the door they'd entered by. Moments later they were on the freight elevator to the city room where they sought refuge in Pete's office.

Bob huffed from his exertion and said between breaths, "Did any of 'em have pitchforks and torches?"

"It did seem like that, didn't it?" Kessler said, as he huffed a bit himself.

Pete was ecstatic. "It was a terrific show!" he said. "I've never seen anything like it. It was raw electricity, a shock wave. You just won over the largest jury the world has ever seen!"

"He's right, Fritz. Mesmer himself couldn't have done it better."

Kessler smiled and said, "It's setting the stage."

"Setting it?" Bob said. "You wrote the ending before the play started."

"I hope so. I always like to know in advance how it ends."

And so the three of them spent the next two hours hiding out while the world outside exploded with news reports, TV bulletins, and pure wonder as they watched the mightiest nation ever reel from the onslaught of a handful of rebels bent on overthrowing the government and, apparently, succeeding.

It happened that the president watched the show even though he later denied having seen it and he wished he hadn't. The mere sight of his antagonist in the first seconds produced a chill up his spine, the same chill he had when he "...wanted to get out of harm's way…" on 9/11 and his mind searched wildly for an updated version of the Air Force One flight to safety.

When the show ended with the explosive shout the president and his accomplices drew back as one and were thunderstruck at the force of it. They looked at each other in awe and confusion, disbelief on every face, outright fear in every eye. It was handwriting on the wall again but this time it wrote their names.

"Jesus Christ!"

"What the fuck was that?"

"Where did he come from?"

The president gathered his wit—he only had one—furrowed his brow to imply thinking, and smirked.

"See? I told you. We should've sent the bastard to Cairo like I wanted. I say we arrest him. Make him confess to helping Al-Qaeda. We could call him a terrorist; say we have proof. I'll issue an Executive Order."

Underling One said, "Great idea, sir!" He snatched up a phone. "Shall I have him picked up?"

Underling Two, not to be outdone, said, "I can have a bag of whips and tongs over here in ten minutes, sir!"

"You could give the bastard a few good licks yourself, sir!" underling Three said. "We all could."

The others nodded and clenched their fists and imagined beating the crap out of the Gray Eminence with expressions on their faces that would have impressed Torquemada in 15th century Spain. The president raised a hand to order the seizure and immediate rendition of Kessler when a fourth underling saved the lot of them a good deal of extra grief.

This individual had just learned that a relative had left him $50,000,000 and he no longer needed any of these assholes including the president so he was free to speak the truth to a man that seldom heard it.

"Sir, I don't think you can do that. The whole world is waiting for the hearing. There will be riots from here to China if you don't give Kessler his hearing."

It was as though someone had just strolled into the temple and kicked old Buddha's gong. A silence both eerie and uncomfortable settled in and stayed as the president struggled to grasp what had just happened, but at least this time it didn't take him seven minutes to get the point.

"And you are…?" he said, using the same tone Torquemada's ax man might use.

"I'm Tupper, sir. You named me that because I once handed you a Tupperwear bowl of Jello in the kitchen."

The president was not amused. "Hmm," he said. He looked at the others. "Not even if I issue an Executive Order?"

Pinned down, they panicked. Underling One had a fainting spell and had to steady himself against the desk to keep from falling over from sheer fright. Number Two assumed a frozen smile halfway between a grinning skeleton and that of a victim facing a firing squad. Number Three put on a brave front and nodded and prayed an earthquake would level the building in the next six seconds.

That left only Tupper, already unemployed but for

the actual formality. He didn't give a damn so he said, "Mr. President, the plain truth is (everyone blanched at the words) there's no way you can avoid the hearing. The political consequences will ruin the Republican Party, they'll lose the Congress for decades, and your legacy will be in tatters."

The president scowled fiercely and number One regained his senses and took number Four by the arm and said, "Come on, Jack, you need to get yourself together." He pulled Jack toward the door.

But Jack wasn't through yet. He resisted being led away and shouted, "Your days are numbered, pal! This place will swarm with so many commoners it'll make Andrew Jackson's inauguration look like a Sunday school romp! The people know who you are now, light out for Nebraska before they tar and feather your ass!"

The distraught man was finally dragged away by guards and soundly beaten just for the hell of it. When questioned later on his yacht, Jack said, "Hey, I got the crap beat out of me, the Secret Service is trying to kill me, and Homeland Security guys have tried to kidnap me twice but it was still worth it, by God! I mean, how many people get to tell the president to kiss their ass?"

Offhand, that would be everybody who votes against him.

Finally, a sounder head prevailed because Jack was right and they all knew it. Arresting and disappearing Kessler was such a stupid idea that even these mugs could see it. The president sighed and settled in to do battle with his foes and let the chips fall where they may.

CHAPTER TWENTY

Of course, the Administration abhorred the thought of giving the rebels a platform and they would normally avoid doing so by stalling and setting up special committees and submitting reports and endless bullshit, but those dodges wouldn't work this time. Everybody knew a delay longer than days would not be tolerated by any of the parties involved so a special bi-partisan committee from both Houses was quickly assembled, Sen. Boris Klench, (R-WY) named Chairman, and an agenda put together designed to make the hearing look more like Kessler's trial than the fact-finding committee it was intended to be. The site was a conference room in the Capitol, the date one week hence.

In one final attempt to exert at least some control of the situation, the White House insisted that the proceedings be closed to the public, no transcripts be made, and all parties be sworn to secrecy. When informed of this last item Kessler gave his opposition a foretaste of what to expect when the fight started.

"Whoever thought that would fly is a fool," he said, laughing. When told it was the president's idea he shrugged and said, "So, the president's a fool."

The quote shot around the world so fast that physicists everywhere thought the message sped faster than the speed of light and the science world was rocked to its core. Foreigners laughed and cheered, stonecutters engraved the words in granite, comedians quoted it in a thousand languages, and a special edition of Bartlett's was issued immediately to include it.

Meanwhile, Bob was still in Colleen's condo and eligible to stay as long as he liked under acquired squatters' rights. With all this renewed activity after Kessler's release he'd become recognizable even to small children and dogs and it wasn't safe to be afoot in the city. That plus the fact that his own place had acquired another media troop to ambush him should he ever try to go home again.

For these and one or two other reasons, Bob dug in with Colleen to wait out the storm so they were on again, so to speak. She went to work every day but he never left the building while waiting for the hearing and it wasn't solely to avoid crowds. Scanlon tipped him off the day after the press conference with a phone call to the Sentinel.

"Ingersoll."

"You on a land line?"

"Yeah, why?"

"It's this. We've got Kessler covered 24/7. Four teams. He's probably got a hundred contracts on his ass already. A lot of people want him dead—and you, too. My advice: go home and stay there until the hearing."

"You really think…?"

"Yes."

Scanlon hung up and Bob kept the phone to his ear for another thirty seconds as though suddenly lost in thought. What did that mean? Hit men? Contracts? Real Gray Eminences plotting his downfall? Why?

Who? Where could he get an armored vest?

Now, Bob was a brave man, a man who could hold his head high and look danger in the eye, but he was also a judicious fellow and not prone to making snap decisions. That's why he hung up the phone and judiciously headed for home without further ado.

Colleen grumbled about houseguests and fish and implied she was making a great sacrifice when she'd come to enjoy his company more each day and was in no hurry to see him go. It was a game where both could be winners or both losers, and not one where either could win while the other lost. Or was it a game at all?

"…and stay home."

"Hit men?"

"That's what he said."

"But…who?"

"He didn't say. Just that these guys want me dead. Remember, it could even be the feds themselves; everybody knows the assholes have no scruples. The Administration would be thrilled if Kessler were knocked off. They wouldn't have to hold the hearing then."

"What if the hit men show up here?"

"Tell 'em I'm not home."

"Will they shoot me?"

"Not unless it's the Mossad. They never leave witnesses."

"What witnesses? I never saw anything."

"Just tell 'em that. They're reasonable guys."

"I've got a better idea."

She rose and went to her bedroom and emerged

moments later with a Smith & Wesson .25 caliber automatic that she held aloft for Bob's inspection. "I'll let these guys do the explaining." She handed him the gun.

"Hey, the Smith & Wesson boys! Nice move. Try to take out the blonde lady first; I think she's the ringleader."

"You said Scanlon's people were protecting Kessler?"

"That's what he said."

"Maybe Kessler should stay home, too. I mean, how do you know the F.B.I. won't provide the hit men?"

"But why would Scanlon warn me then?"

"Maybe he doesn't know himself. They'd double cross Mother Teresa if she got in the way."

Bob sat up at this point and looked at her. "Holy shit, you may be right! I never thought of that." He leapt up and grabbed the phone. "I'm going to give Kessler a heads-up before he finds out the hard way."

He punched in the number. "Fritz? Bob here. You okay?"

"Yes, I'm fine. Why do you ask?"

"Look, maybe it's nothing but Scanlon warned me today that I may be a target for unknown, uh, people. He told me to stay home until the hearing. I was telling Colleen about it and we agreed it could be the feds who are trying to kill both of us. Bottom line: you can't trust any of 'em. Not the Bureau, not Scanlon, not the Administration. So don't go out. Don't let anybody in. Stay put for the next five days."

"Hmm. You may be right. I've thought the same thing myself. It's a bit chilling to think your protectors might conspire to kill you."

"It's the oldest trick in the book, Fritz. Ask any head of state."

"You're right. It's house arrest for both of us."

"It may be a false alarm but you've got the biggest case in our history. I'd hate to see the evildoers win this one—and they will if you don't show up."

"And that might blow your Pulitzer, Bob."

"Hey, this is all about saving America and honor and clean government…"

Kessler laughed. "I know it is and you'll get that Pulitzer. We just have to stay alive long enough."

"Just for five more days."

"Yes."

They hung up and Bob turned to Colleen. "Can you stand me for five more days?"

"Let's do one at a time."

"Yeah."

She snuggled against him and he put an arm around her and they started on the first day.

Although there was a great clamor for Kessler to give interviews and make himself available, both he and Bob remained in hiding for the entire five days and didn't resurface until the morning of the hearing. While no attempts on their lives were ever made it is likely that such attacks might easily have occurred during that period that were thwarted without available targets.

In the interim the country and world were abuzz with excitement as arrangements were made for the hearing. The site chosen was a large conference room in the Capitol building with seating for 110 spectators and a dozen seats on the raised dais for Committee members. The well had long tables facing the dais with seating for witnesses, attorneys, et al., and room for cameras and technicians to record the event. It would be televised worldwide although the White House never actually said so lest it renew another round of jokes in re the president's new semi-official position as an acknowledged fool.

CHAPTER TWENTY-ONE

And so it was that on a bright sunny morning
in July the principal players in the ongoing drama
began to assemble at the appointed place and hour
to decide the fate of the nation. Limos glided back
and forth ferrying the mighty to the fray while lesser
lights arrived in cabs and on foot. Soldiers in full battle
gear were everywhere with fixed bayonets and stern
visages and untold numbers of undercover cops made
up at least 10% of those gathered in the streets around
the Capitol.

Snipers crouched in open windows, security
cameras recorded everything that moved, key players
were ushered into the building surrounded by human
shields of guards paid to take bullets to spare their
precious cargo. No account of the number of rebels
in the area was ever supplied but it's safe to say they
were there in force to make sure the proceedings went
as planned.

Kessler arrived in an armored Humvee followed
by another with business-like machine guns held at
the ready by recently returned Iraq vets while biker
cops coasted along on all sides wearing armored vests.
It wasn't that the authorities were so anxious for a
successful hearing as much as it was the knowledge
that a last minute assassination of the star player
would result in an all-out firefight and convince the
world that the Administration was responsible. Better
to play out the hands dealt and hope to befuddle

everybody with bureaucratic bullshit and feats of political legerdemain that would astonish a roomful of professional magicians.

Of course, Kessler had a plan, too, one that would prevent his opponents' plan from working while his own carried the day.

Once inside, the room bustled with media people in the well and aides on the dais scurrying about fulfilling the wishes of the panel members who were already seated and girding their political loins for the fight of their lives. Kessler sat at the witness table with attorneys Kelley and Keene on either side while Bob sat directly behind him. While not a principal in the proceedings, he was regarded as a witness and subpoenaed to be present should anyone have questions for him. Needless to say, Bob was covering the story from a ringside seat that any reporter would trade his Pulitzer for.

Sen. Klench was a portly man with enormous jowls and tiny eyes. He'd been elected to the House in '76 and to the Senate in '84 and had the enviable record of having been indicted only once for bribery. He won by bribing a juror who hung the jury at 11-1 for conviction and a mistrial resulted. There was additional talk about how he'd amassed a fortune after arriving in D.C. as a penurious freshman but his partners in crime refused to investigate further for fear they might start a trend and they'd end up in durance vile themselves.

The action began when Chairman Klench tapped on his mike and declared the hearing open for business.

"I want to welcome y'all to this hearing on, uh, to look into the, uh, matter of the recent uprising that's caused so much trouble for everybody. In brief, the folks who call themselves rebels want to make changes in how our government works and the president has graciously decided to hear their case to examine its merits." He gestured at Kessler. "Mr. Fritz Kessler is the attorney for the plaintiffs and their leader and he will speak for them during this hearing."

Atty. Kelley raised his hand. "Objection, sir. Mr. Kessler is not a member of the rebel faction; he acts as their attorney only."

"Well, sir," Klench intoned, "that is a question before this Committee. Exactly what is Mr. Kessler's role in these proceedings? Mr. Kessler, folks don't know a lot about you and their curious. We all are. So, I'd like to take a few minutes at the outset to find out exactly who you are and what your role in all this is. Would that be all right with you?"

The Gray Eminence nodded and said, "I have no objection, sir."

Klench shuffled papers and cleared his throat.

"Well, sir, you are an attorney then?"

"Yes."

"Where did you go to law school?"

"Wayne State University in Detroit."

"I see. That's not a distinguished school, is it?"

"It is now."

"Hmm. And you practiced law in Los Angeles?"

"Yes. I had a civil practice. I sued business people and corporations."

"And was your practice successful?"

"Yes, in many ways including financially."

"Hmm. Have you ever been arrested?"

"No."

"Disbarred?"

"No."

"Did you serve in the military?"

"Yes. I was a Marine platoon leader in Vietnam."

"Ever run for political office?"

"No."

"What is your party affiliation?"

"You know you can't ask that question, Senator, but I'll answer it, anyway. I am of the Democratic persuasion because it has always been the party of the people and I'm one of them."

"Are you saying the Republican Party isn't the party of the people?"

"It's a statement of fact. When is the last time you voted for a bill that benefited the poor at the expense of the rich?"

The Chairman's scowled and snapped, "Sir, I'll have you know that I've long supported programs to help poor folks…"

"Name one."

"What? How dare you, sir! I've never seen such effrontery. I'll ask you to keep a civil tongue when speaking to a member of the United States Senate!"

"So, you can't name one?"

"Mr. Kessler, I should remind you that I'm not the one who is on trial here!"

"I should remind you, sir, that I am not on trial here. In point of fact, it is the government that has been charged with high crimes and misdemeanors and must answer to the American people. You and all of Congress are the defendants in this case for violating the laws of the Constitution of the United States and the Declaration of Independence."

At this point, Rep. Rath (R-TX) leaned in and said, "Mr. Kessler, you are very close to showing contempt of Congress…"

"I haven't begun to show my contempt for this Congress, sir."

"Sir," Klench bellowed, "I could have you arrested on the spot…!"

"But you won't."

Senator Hicks (R-VA) said, "Gentlemen, let's focus on the business at hand. We were gaining some insight into the defendant's…I mean, Mr. Kessler's background and we need that information to help us reach a verdict…er, I mean, decide the merits of the case."

"Mr. Chairman," Rath said, "may I take a few minutes of your time?"

"Yes, all right," Klench growled. He stared malevolently at Kessler and gritted his teeth.

"Mr. Kessler, how did you know Mr. Ingersoll?"

"Only through his column in the Sentinel. We had never met prior to the death of Sen. Biggers."

"Why did you choose him as your contact person?"

"We think alike. He cares about the little guy, working people, the ones without health insurance or lobbyists. What's more, I like him."

"Was Mr. Ingersoll ever a part of the rebel organization to your knowledge?"

"No, and there is no organization."

"No organization?"

"No."

"And you are not the leader of the rebel cause?"

"There is no leader."

"How do you communicate?"

"An occasional e-mail or maybe a phone call to arrange a meeting."

"These meetings. How often did they occur?"

"There were some 200 meetings over four years."

"Who set them up?"

"Those who attended earlier meetings recommended me to friends. An e-mail or two or a phone call was our only communication."

"How many would attend a typical meeting?"

"It varied from a dozen or so to several hundred."

"Where did you meet?"

"In private homes, clubs, rented halls."

"Who came to these meetings?"

"Americans concerned with the future of their country. They were professional people, workers jobless because of outsourcing, minimum wage workers with full-time jobs and living below the poverty level, people protesting our foreign policies and illegal war, students. They were all colors, sizes, religions, political parties, and they were all scared."

"What did you talk about at these meetings?"

"You. Your broken promises, your voting record, your unexplained wealth, your support for an illegal war, your…"

"I meant, did you discuss plans for overthrowing the government?"

"No."

"Just no?"

"I answered your question. There was never any subversive talk, no bomb making lessons, no secret arms caches, no mention of violence."

"But somehow they decided to start killing innocent politicians…"

"There is no such thing as an innocent politician."

"But they did start killing people in different parts of the country all of a sudden. Was that by coincidence?"

"It was not planned because there is no plan."

"Then how do you account for..?"

"Sir, the so-called rebels are patriots and love their country so much they're willing to risk their lives to save it from tyranny, greed, and treason. No one needs to tell them anything; they see it plainly enough for themselves. They've decided the only way to assure real reform is at the barrel of a gun. Most of them happen to have guns in spite of the trashing of the Second Amendment and they're using them to shoot their abusers."

"You support the Second Amendment, sir?"

"Of course."

"But you say you're a Democrat and they're against the Second Amendment. How do you explain that?"

"Because they're idiots. The Second Amendment is crystal clear and can be understood by any nine-year-old. The Amendment only has twenty-seven words in it and twenty of them have just one syllable. Why do we need a judge to explain it to us? Until the law is changed the American people have an unconditional right to bear arms and that right cannot be infringed. If opponents don't like it, let them amend the Constitution, but until they do they should stop claiming it says something it does not."

"But certainly…"

"Besides, there is more involved here than the gun issue. The greater fear is the distortion of the meaning of the Constitution. If one can change black to white with the Second Amendment one may do the same with the rest of that document and alter its very nature. That path leads to torture, illegal wars, and true loss of freedom."

"Are you a member of the National Rifle Association?"

"No, but I support their position on the Second Amendment."

Rep. Rath realized he was making little headway and changed the subject. "So, you say your meetings were always peaceable and legal?"

"Yes."

"The rebels acted independently, without direction?"

"Yes."

"I understand you have a list of demands?"

"I do."

"Where did you get them?"

"From topics we discussed at our meetings. They came from many individual meetings because they strike a responsive chord with fellow Americans across the land. People are scared and angry; they resent tax breaks for the rich and higher taxes for them. Yacht sales are up and so are bankruptcies, home foreclosures, and poverty families. One doesn't need a written agenda to know what issues will come up."

"So, you claim your groups were nothing more than a mere debating society?"

"Only if you would call town meetings mere debating societies."

"You never thought there was anything wrong in holding these meetings?"

"Of course not. The First Amendment gives us the right to free speech and assembly. That means we can meet where we like and say whatever we like. Or did the Administration cancel them when I wasn't looking?"

The questions continued in this manner until a break for lunch and Kessler let them go on because he felt the viewers had a legitimate right to know who and what he was and also to firmly establish his role as the rebels' attorney. He knew if the feds found any scrap of potential evidence they'd sign him up for their rendition program.

For many lunch meant standing in one spot for the next ninety-minutes because the room and halls were so packed with humanity that movement was almost impossible. Security tried to clear some space but each new space vanished as soon as they turned away to make another one. Several people fainted but were held upright by their neighbors and thus avoided injuries from falling.

Bob and Kessler followed the Committee through a rear exit and made their way to a nearby restaurant where they conferred with their lawyers over lunch.

"...well, don't you?" Keene said.

"Perfect," Kelley agreed. "It's obvious they don't

have a clue. It's an elaborate fishing expedition; they're not even sure what they're looking for."

"It's a shutout," Bob said. "They haven't laid a glove on you, Fritz."

"I'm not surprised. There isn't much to go on."

"You're going ahead as planned then?" Kelley said.

"Yes. That's what this is all about. We have to win in this arena; we want it to end here without more fighting. All-out war is unthinkable; we already did that."

"A straight answer, boys," Bob said. "What are the odds that the rebels can pull this off?"

Keene threw up his hands. "Fifty-fifty?"

Kelley said, "A guess? The feds will fight hard because they're fighting for survival. I'd say maybe 3 in 10."

"Alone zero," Kessler said. "But with hundreds of millions of supporters and right on our side, I say success is assured. We will absolutely change the course of the nation and this will be a true democracy, the sort of government intended by the Founding Fathers." He paused and looked at his companions. "We're making history, gentlemen. This is a very special moment in the history of the world."

The others assumed a serious mien and nodded and clenched fists and shared a moment that would be forever etched in their memories. Then they tackled more pragmatic matters and turned to their menus.

The afternoon session was a replay of the morning session with Kessler patiently fending off Committee efforts to find a weakness they could exploit to their advantage. Kelley and Keene littered the conference

table with assorted legal documents and conferred
with Kessler but most of it was for show as the Gray
Eminence was leagues ahead of his inquisitors and
never in trouble.

However, although things went well for Kessler he
hadn't yet started on his own presentation that would
focus on the real purpose of the hearing, i.e., the rebels'
demands for a new government.

The first day ended with the groundwork laid in
preparation of Kessler's turn to run things. Bob hitched
a ride in Kessler's Humvee and was dropped off at the
Sentinel where he arrived as a conquering hero. Where
he'd planned to write his column he ended by writing
nothing, as the clamor and confusion created by the
day's events made work impossible. He used the rear
entrance to meet Colleen down the street where she
picked him up and went home.

They ordered out that evening and ate Indian fare
with parantha and lentils and curry everywhere and
Bob rehashed the hearing while Colleen listened and
neither thought of squatters' rights or rent due or what
it's like to eat dinner alone.

After dinner, they carried glasses of Merlot to the
living room where they shared some Purple Haze and
each other and enjoyed a perfect ending to the biggest
day in either's life.

Bob smiled a warm smile and said, "My, that's
good herb."

"It is, isn't it? Light and heavy at the same time."

"Yeah, it's like that old saw, one can be too light for
heavy work and too heavy for light work."

"At the same time?"

"Uh, yes. It involves quantum mechanics and is, uh, very technical."

"But my light and heavy isn't real. I mean, it's only a perception. What would you call that?"

"Stoned."

Colleen laughed and said, "This is good herb."

"It sure is."

They kicked back, feet up, watched a movie, and fell asleep in each other's arms.

The next day all assembled for round two with the entire world on hold. Whole countries essentially shut down for what they knew would be the grand finale and nobody wanted to miss it. Every newspaper had someone ready to race through the city room to stop the presses, anchors huddled with mikes at the ready, pundits sharpened their punds. There would never be another news event quite like this one and everyone knew it.

The Committee had a plan to dazzle Kessler with footwork and bullshit and move the hearing into more of a quest for a political solution with vague promises and demagoguery. While this form had worked for centuries heretofore, it was destined for failure, as Kessler's own plan called for him to take charge of things at this point.

Chairman Klench scowled at Kessler and said through clenched teeth, "We will resume where we left off yesterday. I believe Rep. Rath was …"

Kessler put up a hand and said, "You had your turn yesterday, Senator. Now it's my turn." He stood and stepped out to move into the well as techs scrambled to make room for him.

"Sir," Klench said, "I must ask you to take your seat. Witnesses are not permitted to…"

Another upraised hand stopped him. "The purpose of this hearing was to examine the rebel cause to see what merits it has, if any. I now propose to spell out the rebels' demands so that the Committee may consider them and look at said merits."

"Mr. Kessler, I must…!"

"Shut up, sir!"

Everything stopped, even time. It's true. Several witnesses asserted that the wall clock stopped dead, hands frozen when the words were airborne. Klench was astounded, mouth open, eyes wide, incredulity stamped on his mug like a holy man caught in flagrante delicto by the entire choir. Security people didn't know whether to do nothing or shoot Kessler.

After one of the longest moments in the history of man, although not actually measurable because time had stopped, Kessler addressed the Committee as a whole.

"Let's have an understanding here. The rest of this hearing belongs to my clients; you are spectators. I've come to tell you what to do, not to ask you what we should do. There will be no studies, fact-finding sub-committees, opinion polls, postponements, or delays. After I've presented my clients' demands the government will have seventy-two hours to accept them in their entirety. If the Administration refuses to do so, my clients will resume their attacks on those most responsible for their plight, i.e., you."

The Committee members hadn't fully recovered from being told to shut up so they were unable to muster any bombast or bluster to respond. Instead, they shrank back in their plush chairs as if expecting actual blows and listened meekly as the Gray Eminence laid down the new law.

"You have lost touch with your constituents, with the people you were elected to serve, and attached yourselves to new masters. You no longer vote for the interests of the people but for those who pay for your vote. You routinely accept outright bribes under the guise of campaign funds, ride private jets for free trips abroad, vote to shut down the ethics committee, pad your payrolls with relatives, and endlessly vote yourselves ever higher salaries while freezing the minimum wage for over a decade.

"More than that you are unscrupulous, without integrity or honor. You lie to the people, demagogue them, deceive them. You pay lip service to patriotism and sell out to Halliburton with lucrative no-bid contracts worth billions. You enter politics penniless and leave with a vast fortune in ill-gotten gains. These actions constitute high treason and you deserve to be punished for them.

"Furthermore, you promote and encourage class warfare with the rich ever more prosperous and the people ever less so. Tax breaks for the rich while millions are without health insurance or a living wage are obscene, even criminal. You outsource our best jobs with your so-called free-trade policies that enrich business and corporate interests at the expense of middle-class America. Is it any wonder that a populace so abused might take up arms against its abusers?

"You rig C.I.A. intelligence reports, lie about

imaginary H-bombs in Iraq, tout weapons of mass destruction, exaggerate the war on terrorism for political gain, and cause the deaths of hundreds of thousands of innocent people and our own troops. These are acts of treason.

"You arrest people and jail them without lawyers or even charges against them. You deny prisoners habeas corpus, authorize torture in direct violation of the Constitution's warning against cruel and unusual punishment, and hold trials in secrecy with military tribunals instead of courts. You essentially scrap the Bill of Rights and warn of the dangers from terrorists when you yourselves are ever more dangerous to our country and its values."

People worldwide were entranced as they watched the leaders of the most powerful nation on Earth being pilloried for their incompetence, greed, ignorance, and overall ugliness. Those in totalitarian societies were astounded to see mere people roundly curse out the head guys and still retain their heads. It amounted to one of the most dramatic and effective lessons on what real democracy is all about and it was a lesson well learned.

But Kessler wasn't through yet. He stopped to sip water, reshuffled his papers, and continued his harangue.

"You love earmarks and pork. You try to scuttle Social Security, privatize willy-nilly, complain about welfare even as you vote new subsidies for favored (bribe paying) industries, deny adequate health care for wounded Iraq War veterans and cut a proposed pay increase for our military from 3.5% to 3% because that's all they deserve."

Kessler stopped here and seemed to gather himself before continuing. He drew himself up, squared his shoulders, and forged ahead.

"I could go on but let me finish with a few sentences from the Declaration of Independence." He held up a copy. "I quote: 'But when a long train of abuses and usurpations, pursuing invariably the same object evinces a design to reduce them under absolute despotism, it is their right, it is their duty, to throw off such government, and to provide new guards for their future security.'

"So that's why we're here. We will throw off such government and build a new one, a better one that serves the interests of the American people and not those of special interests. And these are the reforms that will bring this to pass."

He pulled a new sheet from his papers, glanced at it, and looked up at the Committee members who sat in cowed silence.

He read from the list.

"These demands are as follows:

1. Effective immediately, the President, his Cabinet, and all staff members will resign their posts and each current Member of Congress will resign his seat. None will be eligible to hold public office again. New elections will be scheduled for January first next.

2. Official salary aside, no elected official shall be allowed to accept any monies or things of value from any source whatsoever. If convicted, said Member will forfeit his position and serve a

mandatory five years in prison.

3. All elections, federal and state, shall be paid for with tax revenues. Candidates will receive a fixed amount and may not use their own monies for elections.

4. All troops shall be brought home from overseas bases at once.

5. Social Security retirement benefits shall amount to no less than $25,000 per annum based on current indices. This amount shall be adjusted for inflation on January 1st of every year. In addition, a national minimum hourly wage of $12.50 shall be mandated at once; it shall be adjusted for inflation yearly. Each time Congress raises its own pay a like raise shall apply to the minimum wage.

6. Congress shall cover every citizen in the nation with a single payer health plan (Medicare) that includes free prescription drugs.

7. All Bills will be limited to a single item; no riders may be attached to any Bill. Earmarks will be illegal.

8. The capital gains tax and the inheritance tax will remain in effect; both shall be raised by ten (10) per cent per annum.

9. Monies required to fund all of the above shall accrue from taxes laid against the wealthiest taxpayers at rates to be fixed by the new Congress."

He stopped and inhaled deeply. "These demands are non-negotiable. Military action against the government will resume in seventy-two hours if these conditions are not met in their entirety."

He stood erect, hands at his sides, head up and a defiant look that said he meant business and was not a man to be trifled with. After a moment the room exploded with cheers and applause and billions of people around the globe cheered and applauded too and waves of energy and enthusiasm swept the planet as people everywhere took heart and imagined such a scene in their own country. It was a grand moment for freedom and justice and fairness and a not so grand moment for the world's politicians, many of whom resigned their seats at once and tried to beat the mob to the border.

CHAPTER TWENTY-TWO

The world waited impatiently, politicians quaked, and the president decided to head for a safe haven in Nebraska but he was told the state had closed and all airports shut down for, uh, repairs. In desperation, he called his Cabinet together for advice but only four of them showed up. The rest had followed his example and flown off in Texas Air National Guard planes to keep out of harm's way.

He smirked at the faithful four and declared his defiance. "I'll never give up," he said, "because I'm the decider. See? I mean, I understand their anger. I know what people want. They want freedom and some people are trying to take their freedoms away. That's what the terrorists want. They hate us for our freedoms. But we've got God on our side. I talk to him every day. That's why I'm the decider. So we won't give up; they can't intimidate me. I say we fight 'em, send in the Marines, poison their wells and burn their barns. Who's with me on this? Who's got my back, eh?"

"Oh, I'm with you all the way, sir!"

"You bet, Mr. President. You can rely on me!"

"Count me in, sir!"

"Me, too!"

So with the unflagging support of what was left of his Cabinet the president dug in his heels and drew a line in the sand. Unfortunately, the four remaining guys all took to their heels that afternoon and the president sat alone in the Oval Office and surveyed the wreckage of his career with dismay.

The stage was set for an all-out civil war and then something remarkable happened that astonished the world and wrote finis to our story. As the deadline approached and no word came from the president, a strange force began to spread over the land and through its people. As the noon deadline drew near people everywhere began to form up in small bands that grew exponentially larger until they gathered in every state capitol and filled the streets in support of the rebels' cause.

But there was something unique about them. Every person came armed with a gun. They carried hunting rifles, shotguns, pistols both large and small, old guns and new ones, some with bayonets affixed and 'scopes and grenade launching capabilities. There were AK-47s, M-16s, .50 caliber machine guns mounted in the back of pickups, automatic and semiautomatic guns and even kids with BB guns. So many wore bandoleers of ammo crisscrossed on their chests that Bob expected Rambo to show up at any minute.

They stood perfectly still, unsmiling, guns at the ready, a silent citizen army sans leaders, sans money, sans direction. Stirred almost against their will to confront their oppressors, they took up weapons and got into cars and buses and trains and converged on the sin centers where the evildoers hung out. They wanted to send a message that couldn't be misunderstood or spun, one that even fools could grasp, and they took their guns along for emphasis.

The images sent worldwide had an enormous impact everywhere. People watched in awe as cameras all over America focused on the millions of citizens confronting their government in a peaceful protest backed up by enough firepower to knock-off all six hundred members of the Light Brigade with a single volley. Their stillness gave a kind of eerie cast to the scene, like those plaster Chinese soldiers one sees standing motionless in endless rows to guard a dead politician of another era.

And so they stood and the president saw them standing and he turned to remark to an aide only to learn he was quite alone. Everyone had gone. He sighed heavily and went out into the Rose Garden to respond to the rebels.

"Uh, ladies and gentlemen, uh… I've seen the people with, uh, I mean, we accept the, uh…terms and, uh…"

It was over! The world had watched as a mighty nation underwent a complete makeover and emerged a wholly different country with new laws, new leaders, and the beginnings of new respect in the eyes of the world.

In fact, other peoples were so impressed with the apparent magic of democracy in action that they formed groups, armed themselves, and politely asked their politicians to run for their lives. It should be added that out of a sense of fair play the voters gave the larcenous bastards a head start.

As a result bright, new democratic governments sprang up on every side and across the globe and all insisted on adoption of our Constitution in general and the New Rules demanded by the rebels in particular and a thousand-year peace settled over the planet.

As for the principal players, agent Scanlon did become Director of the F.B.I. chiefly because he refused to shoot Kessler in a phony escape attempt. Kessler always appreciated that.

Director Slinker lost his head along with the others and was last seen as a city cop patrolling a beat in a Los Angles barrio as gangbangers hooted and jeered.

Editor Schevo won a Pulitzer Prize and became editor of the New York Times and a popular player in the Big Apple for many years.

All politicians driven from office fell on hard times and suffered fierce attacks of boils, as God wreaked vengeance on them en route to that looming boat ride across the River Styx in Death's trusty bark.

The president resigned and was never heard from again. Plans for his library were downgraded to a single shelf in a storeroom in the Library of Congress. His concern with his legacy proved needless when historians unanimously agreed not to provide one, as the whole thing was just too awful and embarrassing to record. The world never forgave him.

The Gray Eminence remembered the kindness of waiter Dennis in the F.B.I. slammer and was as good as his word when he had him promoted to head kitchen manager at a fat salary with a private slot in the parking garage. He then retired from public life and devoted himself to kindness and good acts and lived out his years as a revered hero and champion of the common man.

Bob won the coveted Pulitzer for his coverage of

the Second American Revolution and sold the movie rights to his follow-up book for $10,000,000 dollars. He married Colleen and she opened her own clothing line and made $50,000,000 dollars or so.

The new president awarded Bob the Medal of Freedom that made him an equal of such luminaries as George Tenet and Jerry Bremer. He later gave it to a one-armed Iraq War veteran he passed on the street.

Finally, grateful judges in Sweden voted Bob the Nobel Peace Prize for his newly launched Pax Ingersoll and he and Colleen lived out their long and prosperous lives in peace and tranquility—and so did everybody else.

THE END

www.ingramcontent.com/pod-product-compliance
Lightning Source LLC
Chambersburg PA
CBHW030923180526
45163CB00002B/448